M000229583

THANKS!
Hope you have as
Much fun reading it...
as I did living it large!!

3-15-21

GERRY BENOIT

FULL

SPEED

AHEAD

SCREW THE SWIMMERS

FULL SPEED AHEAD

©2020, Gerry Benoit

All rights reserved. This book or any portion thereof may not be reproduced or used in any manner whatsoever without the express written permission of the publisher except for the use of brief quotations in a book review.

ISBN: 978-1-09834-143-5

ISBN eBook: 978-1-09834-144-2

To my late brother
Conrad Benoit

'Mister Entertainment'

~PAX~

ACKNOWLEDGMENTS

To my best friends and family. I cannot tell you how many times I was told to 'write the book' by a customer, family or a friend, this is for you.

My brother CW, the stories of a lifetime of fun and to whom I shared a room with growing up, there could be many more books coming. Thank You, now one of my angels.

My fantastic parents Dot and Con, missed, but always part of the future with your memory so brightly shining every day.

Eddie Vallee for playing, 'the guitar' to get life going again. Thanks for your help and support over the last decade to make things work out, and for all the entertainment along the way.

Steve Ferreira for all the technical support to get this project off the ground with the 'electronic push'! Food delivery during the pandemic will never be forgotten, never mind the phone conversations for a laugh.

JC Carreira, found out about the project, and then jumped in to add awesome technical assistance to make this happen.

All the material in this book is my original work and some of the names have been changed to protect the innocent. Any content that by any chance would be in question will be understood that would be the conception of the author which no one else would hold rights.

All rights reserved! No part of this book may be used or reproduced, stored in a retrieval system, or transmitted in any form by any means without prior authorization in writing, except in the case of brief quotations, reviews, and articles. For any other permission contact author.

Special thanks to Margo Calpin for all the moral support and being the wind in my sails.

Kevin Noyes you could not have been in this, thanks for the pushes along the way for more chapters.

Matt O'Connor I will say without your step into my life, it could not have been the same, thanks! With stage and lights, you became a great performer along our side no matter what.

The reading club, thanks for the input. Hundreds strong, and others asking for it, made it real fun to write.

Any events slightly or loosely related to anything in this book hold no claim to this project.

To everyone that followed 'PAX', you were the engine to the performances, we did it for you!

Thanks, Earl Fox, for the positive motivation and drumming advice, and for being the best damn friend my brother CW had! Thanks for his eulogy, no one else could have done it. Perfect!

PREFACE

FULL SPEED AHEAD is a compilation of random life events not in any life order. Every chapter will take you on a different journey. Experience a fun life growing up with great dogs. Get near some fire, and fireworks along the way. Learn how hood surfing was one of the crazy events of our youth. Take some motorcycle journeys that will make you go hum, others that just make you realize your angels 'had' to be there. You will be blown away by a drift, if not by aircraft that have 'issues'! Come live the fun of playing drums in a band for decades with a perfectionist brother. Yeah maybe that had something to do with the Hit Job! Life is fun and fast lived but when toxic relations happen, uh oh! The remarkable part of life is when it comes fast and fun and you lived to talk about it. Enjoy the, oh no it's 'You Again' moments and memories with good old friends that still make them laugh until they cry still thirty and forty years later. Come for the 'Fireworks' of life's display, oh yeah, it was a fun time. Just remember hit that throttle it's, *FULL SPEED AHEAD*...Screw the Swimmers!

TABLE OF CONTENTS

PIPELINE
PROOF OF THE THIRD RAIL

OUCH! Another three stooges prank on me! That's what sharing a room with older siblings was like! That will be another chapter. My brother, CW was a self taught guitar player. For a young teen, as it turns out he wasn't all that bad. His old tube amp of choice, a Fender Twin. That amp delivered a particular sound. The exterior of the cabinet had this certain beige plaid look to it. The corners had nice finish with metal pieces. Yes, this amp was made to be used for the long haul. Etched in my memory is the 'pop' sound it made when that rear toggle switch got flipped, and it came to life. As we grew up that amp was just part of my being because CW never stopped playing through it. I was dreaming of being taught how to play guitar by him as well, but every time he just reneged. On Saturday afternoons we would get dropped off at a music store in Fall River. The owners of Hall's Music store liked to have the aspiring new musicians to the area come hangout and play instruments all day. Maybe one of these kids would be a big star someday. Who could tell, but they would be laying claim to finding them for sure. CW would sit there and play guitar for hours. Tony, one of the owners, played guitar incredibly. He would show my brother tips, as he was a flamboyant guitar teacher as well. When CW progressed, he bought a beautiful Country Gentleman guitar that he just loved. He played it until he wore the finish off. I remember him taking it apart for hours, figuring how to make it work differently, and he did! Nice sounds.

Every time CW plugged in any guitar the first thing he would do was slide down the neck doing a riff from a tune by the Ventures ~ 'Pipeline'. Not sometimes, but every time! I just got used to it, but he would adjust the amp after that little ditty to his liking that minute for what he was thinking. A few seconds of tuning, really, just always that fast it seemed. I think he must have had the tone in his head. A vast amount of times I saw him strike a tuning fork, then put it between his teeth. He said it drove the correct sound through your head! I had to believe him, how the fuck would I know, I was just a young kid. Time flies, I finally got to play the drums and sing behind my brother in a band he created that would thrust him into playing bass. The band was 'PAX'. We only had three people that ever played with us in the core of the band over its illustrious career. Nino, would be with us for years on guitar. He finally gave it up because driving school buses, and five to seven gigs a week for years beat him up! The next, Lonesome Lenny, joined us on guitar for another long stint, keeping my brother on bass. The last to come was Matt. My brother had met Matt on some country gig as a fill in. CW would take my drums to go play on a night our band wasn't playing. Like he said, playing is better than sitting home. Then, I'd bitch about him using 'my' shit! My first memory of meeting Matt was in my parents garage. I was working at a car lot by day and doing all the gigs the band would take. Sometimes back then your employer actually understood when you were doing the band stuff. You just had to make them come to one of the gigs, and bingo, you had them sold!

Closing a closer with the great demo, yeah it always worked! Every single time you had a gig from then on they never stopped you. They became great fans!

The beginning of Matt's chapter started with a page phone call at the dealership. It's tagged a 'family' call! Oh boy, I never get these, what could this be? I think I ran 20 catastrophes though my head as I ran to my office. It was CW on the other end. Hey you plaid suited car salesman you gotta get to the house right after work tonight. I will have your drums set up, we have some pressing news. A new guy starts Wednesday so we have to work this out. Normally this was a night for me to go to see a great local big fifteen piece jazz band. The huffs and puffs of protest were coming out from me you can rest assured. After the sound in CW's voice, being called an asshole, then having my life threatened for several minutes, yup, be there at eight fifteen.

It was a rare occurrence when we would practice. If we did, within a half an hour of start and stops on one song, I'd snap! CW and I would be in some kind of wild issue that the third guy wouldn't understand. Unless you work with a sibling with perfection issues, you wouldn't know the scene. As I walked into the garage of my parents house, I couldn't believe the whole band setup was ready to go. The different thing about the sight was CW's guitar amp ready, and his Telecaster leaning against it. The new dude is playing bass?! Holy shit, a lightning storm in my head! I hadn't seen my brother with a guitar in hand for years, this was going to be interesting real quick! First thing I heard when he strapped that guitar on, ~Pipeline~! As usual he always did it! The new guy Matt was much younger than us and nice guy. Big question running through my mind was, the youth factor. How could he know the gig? We did music much older than I was thinking his normal gig to be. After some friendly greetings and naturally grabbing a beer to try this kid out, we got into it. Three songs stopped 20 times and my brother kept showing him where the songs were going. I was in total panic inside thinking this thing will never fly by Wednesday, no way! An hour into it was too painful for me, I had to go. I said, "good luck by Wednesday getting a whole gig into this guys head." I must say, his fingering was perfect on the bass, and without doubt he could play. He was not a singer, that wasn't good, we had pride in being a vocal band, and wanted to keep it that way. CW saw something I couldn't have in Matt, I'm glad he did!

My next phone call from my brother found me in my office while writing up a car deal. We were on speakerphone listening to CW and Matt doing the gig without my drums or vocals. I think in my years of the car biz, it was one of the most fun deals I ever did. So when the call ended my customer asked what that was about. After a real quick rundown, he was asking the address of the club the next night. The fact that a speaker phone call made this guy say, "that was awesome" made me have hope for the next night! He and his wife showed for that gig, and followed us for years after it. On the stage that nite was some crazy stuff being yelled to me, and at me by my brother. I sang songs I had never had a chance to do before. The whole time listening to my brother singing other songs at me from the side to screw me up. To this day, I don't know how he could play one song and sing a totally different one at the same time! Damn! That night also as I remembered him plugging the guitar in, and I heard it. That same riff as always. Why? Just a habit, the reverb, the sustain? I never really would know ..... For many years Matt played with us and became a great entertainer, singer, lead and backup. It was always fun when he would sing 'Long Cool Woman'. During the beginning riff, and during solos, Matt would jump up on corner side of my drum riser to launch off for some effect before he'd jam into the lyrics of the song! Great for the show, and fun for us too. Over the years it just became so fun it was part of us, and always kidding about the band was worth more. More, yeah we came with lights and our own stage, be it only for the drums. I stole the idea from the famous Earl Fox, a lifelong friend of my brother. Actually he was my brother's drummer until I showed up, uh oh! Earl could drum his ass off, he didn't sing, or I would have never had a chance! Every time I screwed up, got hurt, or while in the service, Earl was always the man! Like I say, whew, thank goodness Earl didn't sing!!!

The band played and had so much fun that sometimes at the end of the gig when CW was paying me, we used to laugh and say, get paid for this too!???! All the many years of fun and games came crashing down one morning, when CW didn't wake up. Many years of bookings to try to fill and no band to do it with, what a mess. Worst part, screw the gigs, my bro! I never had time to do the right grieving thing, with parents snapping over loosing their first born. We were struggling to make sense of a real life kicking our ass. I never depended on any day job, playing in that band was more to us than anything. Now life was going to get interesting. A short while after that, Matt moved his young family to Michigan. That is another quick chapter, or book for a later date.

I met Eddie, a fantastic guitarist one Saturday night in Portsmouth, Rhode Island. The one thing a band guy doesn't like to do that plays full time, is be seen out on a weekend. It means your not gigging! This night, I finally got to talk with Eddie at break. I came to see this band when ever we got canceled, they did big band stuff. That band still performs today. Eddie was a slamming guitar player! I grabbed his card and asked if he would come do some flavorful add leads on one of our big gigs. Musicians being who they are, always want to play. I did say, great cash, oh yeah, that could have something to do with it. As things would be, shortly thereafter we lost CW, and Eddie and he never met, what a bummer. I found out later they may have. All master guitarists in this whole area took lessons to learn great theory from this guy Red. Red played guitar in the big band era and taught theory. So there could have been a day my brother met Ed at Red's. Our past player Lenny went there, and so did several other great guys I met over the years. Eddie and I still to this day are as close as brothers.

Years that went by after CW's passing would be very interesting, to say the least. I tootled around playing in a friend's band to replace someone they were not interested in playing with anymore, a chapter for later. I did construction after blowing out of the car biz, which definitely left too much time on my hands. One thing that kept happening though, was certain things that make you go hummmm. Every time I heard 'Long Cool Woman' on the radio, within three hours Matt would call from Michigan. I know he doesn't get the same radio we do there, but it kept happening! Not sometime, this one was turning out to be true every time. I didn't know whether to be freaked out. Instead I just always thought it to be CW tapping on our shoulders from the other side! Yeah, I just said it.

Time was clicking by, and I was out to see the band Eddie was playing in very often. I did a few minor repairs at his house from time to time. We would do a minor repair, then drink the day away and usually talk about crazy deep thought shit. The jokes would be crazy, continuous, and it was always a fun time. The subject came up one day about playing my late brother's favorite guitar. Ed didn't really sound too interested but was kind of humoring me by saying he would. Great, I made a meeting with him at that jazz club I liked on Monday nights, and brought the guitar for him to see in the trunk. We watched the band for a set and then time to shift on out, being a work night. Time to see if he likes this thing. I'll never forget the sight on Eddie's face when I opened that trunk and a '72' Telecaster was in there! "Whoa" he said, "whoa hell yeah I'll play that mother! Gerry! What 'da fuck?!" My favorite line! Now I couldn't wait until Wednesday night to see him play at a casino in Connecticut. I knew he'd play that Telecaster like it was an assault!

A few hours later Eddie called me to ask if the guitar was haunted, a music box in his house that was known to be broken, played! His wife Paula, was freaked out! I think they enjoyed their drinks that night, after Eddie was made to put the guitar in the car's trunk, in the garage! The next day I was working on a church in Lincoln, Rhode Island. I called Ed and was telling him how hearing the signature sound of that guitar would be like hearing my brother play again. I remember getting every one ready to be off the job on time, if not early that day. I wanted to get home, throw food down, shower, and get to that casino.

The drive to Connecticut was filled with excitement to go see a band I had seen a thousand times, but this one was gonna be different. Walking in from the parking garage, the band was getting ready for sound check. As I got to the stage, Eddie was using his tuning device. "It's in tune! Are you kidding me?"

He said, "brother it's in tune, how long has it been?" I'm thinking if this thing is in tune after thirteen years, then, yeah it wants to be played! The band was as awesome as usual. I will say this, Eddie played a few riffs he never used to play, it always makes you wonder. He and I were to discuss that at the end of the night. We believed CW was happy to hear that instrument play again, did he help, or influence? Not for us to know, we have no right to that third plane we're not privy to.

The next day, as planned the night before at the casino, I showed at Ed's house to do a few small repairs. A bite of lunch then time for stories and drinks. Ed would fiddle with whatever guitar he'd pick up, which usually ended up as a bunch of laughs with a few old musicians, go figure. This turned out to be interesting though. He brought out an amplifier a friend Jim had just restored. I couldn't believe my eyes. It was that same fender twin amp my brother always had in our room. "There's nothing like one of these", Ed says. "I love this damn thing, well let's put it this way, there's only two names in my checkbook, Jim's and my daughters!" At that point I mixed some more drinks while he set up the amp. I came over with the drinks in Ed's great room as the amp got plugged in, and then, out it came, the Telecaster!

We sat there for a minute talking about the normal crazy shit and had a few sips. Then he got the amp popped on with the Telecaster connected. A few more laughs and as both of us had one side of these huge leather couches laughing drinking, he grabbed the bitch and you couldn't believe the first thing that he did. Could this be? 'Pipeline'!! Holy Shit! I said, "that's the first thing that guitar played every time my brother plugged it in! I can't believe you just did that!" The hair stood up on my arms.

As if that weren't crazy enough, my phone rang. It was Matt calling from Michigan! "Hey brother what's going on, the urge to call just hit me, I'm working in a bank, ha, a bank job", as he laughed. Matt had heard about Ed a bunch of times over the years, and vice versa, but neither had met. "Matt", I said "I'm here with Eddie, I just worked on his house, now we're drinking, telling jokes and he was just going to play CW's guitar at his house. He pulled out the same amp CW had our whole life, then did the little ditty! Tell Ed, you're on speakerphone, what CW did every time he plugged in his guitar."

Right away without delay Matt says, "that ~Pipeline~ riff!" So here we were, 13 yrs after he had passed, still grabbing people by the shoulder, making them play this, that, or the other, or, just make that call!!! It was that third rail we are not allowed to know about.....being part of the ~Pipeline~ of communications from ....where??

As the day went on and the stories of premonitions had in the past that came true went on. I could not believe some of the things I saw that happened years ahead of time. The conversations went on until the one, I hadn't seen true yet, was very disturbing as others were that got discussed. It was about a weaponized pandemic that had been launched against this country and most of the world, but with us totally in mind. It was an hour and a half recitation of things I saw, and who I thought would be behind it, and the multi nations involved, and the reasons I thought why they thought they had to do it. Eddie was one of the best listeners I have ever known, because I think as I was talking about it he could see the stubbornness of different people, countries, and was picturing the sickness involved. As we went further, the financial aspect was talked about because these different countries hate us so much and how they were after our manufacturing and different parts of our economy. Thank goodness for his wife getting home and the whole subject changed to eating some quick dinner so I could get home to the dog.

So I sat here this week. The first two days I had to come home from work because of a severely compromised immune system, freaked out! A few months ago, they launched it the bastards. I have to say that with a blind eye to it all, our congress was too busy impeaching the president to pay any attention to any world affairs. Part of the problem was some of the bad players at the World Health Organization, acting in conjunction with these fucked up countries that hate us!

The phone call came Saturday from Eddie. He asked me if I remembered the day at his house going through it all. It was 2008, so, here ya go again, this one was twelve years since I discussed it with him but it was thirty years since I had originally saw it, waking me up from a sound sleep one night with a cold sweat! When Nine Eleven happened I thought that could have been it. Too much didn't match up or make sense, so I didn't quite seem to believe that was it. The call the other day though made me think again.......is there a ~Pipeline~ we just can't touch, it's all around us, they are around us, I hope they protect us.

The guitar made it's way around the eastern seaboard with Eddie playing it. She finally came back home to hang displayed in my fabulous pool room with the rest of his instruments. Pictures of us all over, and the three different versions of the band are in that room. A great picture of Earl playing drums in the band while I was away in the service, standing while playing Wipeout! He made it different for sure, he was an animal. I have picture proof! But wait, there's more! Earl's son became a famous artist, and Brian's work is all over the room too! There are sleds we got on my sixth birthday Christmas morning hanging on the walls, catchers masks, mitts, ski's used growing up, drumsticks used on special gigs hanging, and some special hunting gear. Custom neon lights displayed, along with a fabulous bell collection my mother had. Sometimes I just sit look around, and listen to my life talk to me in that room. How could you not, with pieces of your life jigsaw puzzle all around you.

Today while letting some scenes from my life flow through my fingers on this darn keyboard, it happened again! Why did the phone ring with Eddie on the line, just seconds after I had first mentioned him in this crazy little thesis just kind of freaked me out. Of course the first effort I made writing this took place back in 2011.

The computer I was using back then was akin to a dinosaur when the zip drive failed and the emails of it to Eddie were lost. It's actually crazy to think it's happening again. This computer is from ten years ago when that last one blew up. Here we go on a rhino again! I told Eddie I was at it again, he told me to just keep writing! Strike two for the day was when the phone rang again after I wrote about Earl! How is it he would be on the line?! Last time I chatted with him was a bad weather morning. He was calling to see if I would be needing help. He had done the same more than a month ago. Again, he was on the phone offering to help with anything I may need. I didn't mention this little thesis or feces to him, depends on who's reading it I guess. It was still though another example on how we have this awesome electrical, mental connection in life. Many calls came yesterday from some old, and fairly new friends. The many conversations were just awesome, some deep, some not so. I guess it's just part of the people above us, shoving things around and tapping us, just making us pick up the damn phone, or text nowadays. The only thing I can think about all this.... they all know about one thing......the ~Pipeline~ !!

RIDING FREE-FALL
NEVER FASTER THAN ANGELS

That weighs three tons, you better not! I have to get under that deck first to make sure the wizard that built it didn't doink something up on the install. It would be just your luck buddy, with fifty six hundred pounds of water, and five or six people to come tumbling down. Even though it was only two feet or so, it would definitely ruin your day! A new big hot tub was being delivered in a few days, but I have to tell you, my plans were to be screaming on my bike toward the car races in Charlotte. Then ride to Key West, I was hoping. If I managed to get on the road early enough I would do the Skyline Drive in Virginia. I had heard from friends and family members that if you ever had the chance, do it!

The next day had me slivering under a deck in the moist Martha's Vineyard sand with some spiders I finally nicknamed. One got named, 'holy shit', just for the sheer size! Another was called, 'you fucking better not be poisonous'! I know it's a long name, but I was visiting their territory, and wanted to make it fast to get this job done, get on that bike, and head outta town! Inspection proved my point, I got hustling under there digging, poured some fast forms with quick concrete, slid in supports and finished better attachments to the house! Done....uh oh, better fast cut these nails on the deck rail for them to quickly remove to slide that heavy puppy on the deck. Yeah, I can already hear the rumble of my bike in my head riding southbound.

The bike ended up getting the full wash and wax job before heading out. There were hand prints all over her from having a brand new set of tires put on, total lube, even put bearings in while the front end was apart. At forty five thousand miles on her, I didn't think that to be such a bad idea. I sat and watched Panhead working on the damn thing it seemed for a lifetime the day before. I remember busting his balls when he was rubbing grease into the bearings, that if he ever rubbed a woman that well, they'd chase him into the flames of hell. We laughed away the day, listening to 'Rush' on the radio. On the wall he had a terrorist card deck from '911' with X's thru the ones that had gotten 'justice' served already! Yeah, some rock 'n roll music, beers, and finally time to go, see ya like in four or so thousand miles after this trip buddy! Yeah don't worry, I know, shiny side up!!!

Packing up the race radio, some clothes, to hell with a lot, I'll buy some out there! I just could not get going fast enough that next morning. As I sat there waiting for the boat I was just imagining the route I was going to take in my mind. I couldn't help daydreaming of some of the race team shops I always visited when heading south. The track, the smells of the races, and friends I was anxious to see. Next, I was driving onto the Islander, a Martha's Vineyard icon. The vessel had been a most dependable one on the scene from the mainland as the connection for decades. It had a New England touch of seagull weathering to it! Probably had a couple hundred coats of paint on her, she always smelled like fresh paint. The big slit doors in the fore and aft were huge with millions of teeth on the huge long rollers that made them work. You knew you were on your way, when you felt those doors get let down onto the deck with a slam, as they let the hydraulics down. It was always awesome if you were first on that boat, not only were you first off, but you sat and witnessed the nice view, and Vineyard Haven Harbor. Well on this day I was first on, the guy calling the vehicles was my brother in law's friend, it was almost a guarantee! I was so excited I didn't even go upstairs, I just leaned against the bike, looked out the window and prayed for this damn boat to go faster!

As the Islander got to the mainland, Tommy, a hot shit I worked with in the past at the same dealership came over. He had left the dealer to come work on these boats, but it was the first time I had a chance to see him. He had a nice bike too, and we talked about some of the crazy shit we had gotten into at the car lot. Finally the doors opened and my friend Tommy gave me the green flag, I was off on my wild tour. I just kept hoping I would get to Key West to skydive, swim, and raise hell, never mind the two weeks, and six races I would be seeing.

I'd like to say riding with the wind in my hair, but so much for the hair, and I wear a helmet. I was blasting on the mid cape highway like I was a State Cop on the way to a call. I think all the cars thought that too, they were dashing over to the right as I slid by. The Otis A.F.B. rotary was fun, whew this bitch is flyin', easy 'Ger'! I had to talk myself down again as I got to the Bourne Bridge Rotary, the Cops were really always there. Nice, coast clear, oh I love the sound of these fish tails on this old Eighty Six Electra Glide Classic Liberty Edition when ya smack that throttle for maximum power! The engine had been bored out lickety split, with double notched pistons and with a screaming eagle chip, oh this frigging thing flew. Yup already to the highway to take me past my hometown area and head me out to Providence, R.I. It seemed like only a song or two on the satellite radio before I was heading under the concrete menace City Hall of Fall River. I headed up the one and only Braga Bridge overlooking my hometown of Somerset. I love this place, wow what a nice unbelievable day, I can see Providence from the top of the bridge, nice!! I wanted to slide by really quick to give my mom a kiss, but knew she'd be sleeping. She was quite the night owl doing cross-word puzzles and TV for sure. I blew off that idea just as fast as it went through my mind, and it was already a left turn at Providence, Rhode Island heading south, yeah baby.

Connecticut seems to take forever cause there are only a few nice vantage points of view on the way. On the return trip my friends, a great restaurant diner I always frequented. I hit New York City at just the right time as planned, so good, because motorcycles and toll booths don't get along! Cars merging on you fast, and long lines to make a Harley overheat are not my world. Today though was a two minute venture at the toll booths, and a wild ride listening to my bitch scream. A nice low, loud, nasty rumble in the tunnels of the Cross Bronx Expressway, yeahhhh, that's my beast! New Jersey is, well what can I say, New Jersey. Don't look for dead bodies off the road at rest areas, then you won't find 'em! Maryland got me to Virginia, where I was about to hit the mountains in record time!

Skyline drive is just a place of wonder. I was riding up a steep curvy winding road, the bike just leaning way over each switch curve the road took. In this deep old forest cover, absolutely huge majestic tree canopies just about blocked all the sunlight of the bright mid day beautiful sky, it was dim lit here. You could smell the moisture of the morning fog that had just burned off, and actually could still be seen in some of the lower valleys. I noticed through breaks in tree cover, a view of how much rise in elevation I had achieved in such a small time. The first stop, to get some of these warmer clothes off, and get going after a nice drink. Starting to change coats became interesting, as everywhere you looked, there were butterflies landing on everything! I noticed it on my helmet I had put on the seat at first, thinking that must be good luck. Then as I started looking at the bike they were on the top of the windshield, the gas tank, just everywhere, it was incredible, again I saw it as a sign from somewhere, it is good luck. Riding a bike, it's always a belief, oh yeah, it's gotta be good! OK, back on the trail. Several of the overlooks were awesome, I love mountain scenery, who doesn't. Then along the way, a minivan from Canada stopped at the same time. Again also, at a few more over-looks coincidentally.

The third time we stopped, I was taking pictures when I met the guy driving the van. While reading the plaque describing what your viewing, he said it was his mom's birthday in the van. She had always wanted to ride on a Harley, and will never get to obviously. I said, "Really!? Let's go, we're getting her out of that frigging thing, she's getting on it, and I'm taking her out at least three more stops for a ride. Buddy, you fucking better get some pictures of this, and don't let her say no!! Watch this!" The next minute, I strolled over to the nice little old gal in the passenger seat of the van. Introductions made through the window were cordial. In the quick conversation to follow, she was excited to tell me about begging to come see relatives in Virginia for her birthday. Her son was being a champ, and making it happen for her. She said she was Ninety! Wow, congratulations and then I sang the 'schmaltzy' bar version of happy birthday to her. I think I sounded like Bill Murray from Saturday Night Live. She had such a hot shit smile going, and then got right to it! She blurted out that one of her bucket list items was always to be a motorcycle mama! I thought it funny, we were all laughing when she said that. She said, "absolutely, no shit, I always wanted to ride a Harley!" I opened the van door and made her get out. I got the extra helmet hidden in the trunk. "Let's go!! Happy Birthday!" We got her on with a little effort, helmet strapped on, then here we go! I started the beast with a nice little roar, gave the son a nod and said, "see ya when we see ya!" It was so fun to listen to the ooh's and ahh's back there as I drove though the next several miles with her. We finally came to a nice level over-look good for the old gal to get off, and great background for their pictures. Pretty fun to have a great time with old people, they enjoy the world so much. Her son was absolutely blown away! She got her wish, mom's are everything!!!! I could just imagine how this guy felt with his 'Harley riding mom' now hey? We then waved goodbye!

As night fell I was still on the Drive, and didn't want to be. Not only steep curves with corners, but the condensation on these roads was kind of like ice, I was hating it. Thinking totally of only road conditions was not really all one could contend with. I had seen so many deer all day long near the road, night was freaking me out. Let's get down off the mountains, and out of the woods boy! A bar, great meal, motel, and hot shower made the next morning look great to me! Now it was the ride to the general Charlotte area to visit all kinds of race shops to see some friends. I loved hooking up also with a race crowd that would all camp together at the track. Seeing the race clan was always interesting, they were a perfect painting of the south. One actually came down from Canada, so I could never claim award for coming from farthest away! They had two Australian Shepherds, a his, and hers, neither to be messed with either! The All Star race was a blast that night, right after waking the next morning, I wished them all adieu. I told them I hope to see them the next week for the big race, in the same spot, for the Coke 600. The promises of home made ice cream of several flavors made for me the next week made me want to return!

South Carolina and Georgia were just an absolute treat to ride through, yeah baby, my goal was Key West now, or bust! Coming into Florida made you realize driving with old people you better just stay in the high speed lane or you die!! A few just went right across in front of me, and flipped me the bird too, ha, I couldn't believe it. One of the bitches of life, is when you hit the Miami area at traffic time, holy shit! Finally, nearing sunset, Key Largo owned the night in my head. Ten minutes later I had the last room at a place right on the water. The guy said at the desk, have yourself out there in a half hour for a great sunset. The Heineken I just bought was going to be premium on my list right away. Then, going out to tend to this sunset. As I headed out of my room I slipped and fell. I went down, and snapped my back out!!!! Holy Shit NO! Riding a motorcycle with an issue in the back, NO! UH OH, more beer! I limped to the beach area like an invalid my goodness, I was like one of three guys. What was with all the chicks? Nice introductions and basically I was the only new one there, after the laughs about the fall and back story, it turned out one of the chicks there worked for the local chiropractor. There I was the next morning, getting a snap in Key Largo. The office building was like a flamingo pink with an articulating sign shooting out smart ass chiropractor jokes, yeah right, they cracked me up too! This guy was the one time snapper...your good, enjoy the Keys. He gave me a card in case I needed him on the way out of the Keys too. Suggestions on what to do further down the Keys was discussed as the bike fired up. He told me of a fishing boat a friend owned, and a biplane tour guy that was a friend, I asked him to set me up with that guy. By the time we were done calling people we had been in his office a half hour. I was all set up with biplane rides, skydiving, and a snorkeling thing, but he told me the real key with that....swim behind her, she's awesome! He was not joking,..... wow!

Riding down through the different Keys, it was just beautiful, the people were really nice. Of course this was their off season, so they were happy to see anyone! A few fast dips by different bridges did it for me too, the water so warm, unlike the Vineyard where you get a major case of shrinkage, if ya know what I mean. The fabulous famous Seven Mile Causeway was fantastic to ride on. There wasn't much traffic at all, so the sightseeing was incredible. The water seemed like you could see the bottom, and all the sand bars so beautiful giving the light aqua shallow areas. Couldn't help but look for the place right away though to do this biplane ride. Oh yeah I see the sign now, Conch Airlines, can't wait to meet this Jim, he sounded fun on the phone.

The next scene has Jim head first down into the front cockpit installing the stick, so I can 'drive the damn thing!' Yeah he's gonna let me drive the damn thing!! It was a beautiful nineteen thirty seven Waco biplane, the same exact one that Howard Hughes had. This one was painted a beautiful deep blue, her name, 'Sweetie Pie'. After a check for communications, and a stern warning, 'don't fucking let your leg hit that stick man', because if I did, it may crash us. Yeah, I think I caught all of that. When he started that baby, it was like the flying bad ass version that my bike was to the road, yeah, that's the ticket! Just taxiing to the runway bumping up and down, and trying to get my fresh battery in my video camera, I had that nervous feeling. Oh fuck here we go! Gonna be an easy glide ride here?

Not with this guy Jim! He screamed, "don't touch that stick now!" Right as we lifted off, you could tell the bumpiness of the grass runway stopped. As I looked out toward the hanger we had just came out of, the earth went away. I was looking down at the sky??!!! When we got to about thirty feet off the ground he went upside down, holy shit, I almost launched my video camera, ahhhhhhhh! Then he went right side up and started climbing, with me screaming! He said to me unless I hit the dash button he couldn't hear me, I hit it, and screamed, "ahhhhhh!" He said he did it just to see if he could scare a Harley guy, oh Fuck yeah buddy, you got me! We flew out by a beautiful island light house. He strafed some people in their boats fishing, you could see their eyes wide open as this biplane comes swooping down within twenty or so yards away. If those people could see how scared shit I was, they'd never believe it. The next thing he wanted to do was stop the traffic on the Seven Mile Causeway. I asked him how he does it, and again I got yelled at, "don't touch the fucking stick or we die!". He went into what stunt plane drivers refer to as 'Lazy 8's', letting the plane make huge loops to the left, and then to the right. Holy shit! Within two seconds, and just for total fear, I kind of closed my legs. Not a great idea when this guy is doing major shit with this plane, "your on the stick you fucker, on the stick on the stick!", he was yelling, until I realized, oh it's me!!! When we came out of that I was scared shit! He did another one and then stopped so I wouldn't puke up his plane, and yeah, the traffic on the causeway was stopping in both directions.

It was time, he flew us out to a point and, "it's yours kid" he said, "take the stick and I will guide you, your flying us back!" A few minutes in, he kept telling me I gain altitude all the time, I thought that funny since, yeah I do. He did use the jokes about it too, getting high and all those innuendos. It seemed like too soon, but we were back doing the runway 'cross flight' before landing, he made me bring it around until about a hundred feet or so from the runway, and took over. He had me scared shit cause he didn't have me aiming on the runway, I was off the side. He knew it though, with this kind of side winds he'd have to what they call, 'crab it in'! With a sideways swoop into the wind he landed that bastard up on two wheels, and snapped it around, and dropped us onto the runway in the opposite direction so fast it made your head spin! I hit the mic and screamed, "hell yeah!" He yelled back and said that he had only wrecked it six times before trying it! The plane rebuilds well and he does all the work! I was thinking, thanks for telling me that now fucker, holy shit! I put the camera back aiming at him, I was doing the intro for the tape, he gave the thumbs up as we were on the taxi back, gave a, "hi mom!" to the camera, thought that was a riot. Jim was just a great, fun guy I would go back and ride with again! Turns out Jim certified the guy who does the biplane flights on Martha's Vineyard. Yeah, islands fifteen hundred miles apart, and a connection!

Next up, a few more miles to ride, from marker seventeen to mile marker ten, Skydive Key West! The guy who owned it was a very thin framed Aussie. The accent was awesome because at my sister's house, Steve Irwin was always the imitation. We all messed with the accent. Getting to see the landing area made you understand why no solo dives allowed at the place. An error one way, power lines, the other way, coral reef, the other direction would be hitting the shack and my bike. None seemed like excellent options, the tandem dive was the only ticket. A quick call to the Aussie's friend brought 'Sun-Man' into the picture. He is a video expert, he does the videos of the guys skydiving with boards and stunting for the 'X' games. I was feeling great about the quality of the videos and pictures for sure. No talking while the chute gets packed was the order, then off to the little plane. Sun-Man's video helmet was awesome. He had two video cameras, one on each side, and a still camera mounted on top with a cable down into his mouth. He uses his tongue to fire off the still pictures. Oh yeah the equipment said it all. They proceeded to get this show on the road. Radio clearance from the air force base was needed for us to get to the altitude were going to.

As the plane was going to the altitude of ten thousand feet with it's spiraling incline, a bit of interplay and fun was going on. I didn't know til later Sun-man would put all that to music! There still my friends, will be no sound like a plane door opening at altitude. It's a sound I got to know, love, and fear all at the same time being in the Special Forces, but at least this was for fun! Bang...as the door opened it snapped up to the top in it's jumping position. The moment was here, and in less than a flash, like a spider, Sun-man was out on the wing backwards holding on and waving to me. What a frigging showoff!! It was definitely one of the best maneuvers I ever saw, and he was out there waiting for us. He dropped backwards, zoomed and flew around us, high fives mid air in Free~fall! There we were, above the cotton ball like clouds under us, looking at the greater Key West area, falling at about a hundred and sixty five miles per hour. If you opened your mouth too much, your face cheeks were like a chipmunk. The speed, and the sound of your wind breaking free~fall like a freight train was acceleration at it's best!! The tap came for all hands in for the canopy blast. Whoom, shoot open, and the sound of nothing! Now it gets so quiet and beautiful, just floating above the most excellent coral reefs and bright white sandy beaches around every one of the Keys. Sun-Man just continued his free~fall and did a death dive so as to video us landing a foot away from his camera. We slid in on our asses right by the helmet cameras. Oh fuck yeah, what a blast!!! Jim and 'Sweetie Pie's' stunts, Riding the Beast, and Free~Falling on the quest to Key West was part of the scene. Riding south and screaming, "It don't suck to be me!!!!"

I entered Key West rumbling down streets slowly doing a head swivel. I love new things and I have to tell ya, it seemed like there were a lot of thumbs up as the bike went by open restaurants and bars. It was like a southern Martha's Vineyard feeling to me, I think it was the friendliness. OK it was time to find a place to stay. The Cypress turned out to catch my eye and it was really close to the downtown scene, perfect, hope it's not a ton of money!! When I walked in the owner was asleep at the desk, so I was thinking this wasn't a high pressure scene. Two seconds of talking with the gentleman had me being shown a nice room with my own toilet! Turned out to be very special there, holy shit! I actually had my own single person spa out there, it was awesome! And a cat. A what? A cat! What's with the cat? Well it was a twenty year old that always lived there, so if it wants to come in or out of that room, let it! Wow, so now I had a room mate! I parked the bike, covered her, locked it up and handed the keys to the guy. I said, "DO NOT give these back until I leave! No matter what I say, lock them up. I plan on getting crazy, don't let me have those keys!" Point well taken they got locked up, he laughed his ass off. He then told me, "watch out for the roosters."

I still had no fucking idea what the 'rooster' thing was about I just wanted to have a shower, a spa, sleep an hour or so, and be on to partying. I got scared out of sound sleep by the cat jumping on me, oh fuck! It must have been hiding under the bed when I arrived, but it was a frigging cool cat! Many drinks, a lot of food with one hell of a sunset. Yup, it was true, the whole town with drinks in hand, head to see the sunset and applaud when it is over every day! A motivational scene actually, what a fun place. Alas it was time to head out. The cat was like a packing buddy as I got all my stuff together, funny stuff. On my way to the bike I found out about the frigging roosters. One with some young tried to take me down, and chased me too. The natives must look and laugh. It's the only indigenous creature of Key West, I would later find out. Let's rumble this baby going North. One last thing to do before going, is take a picture with the Southernmost Point of the USA marker with me and the bike. I thought important, not everybody rides to Key West from Martha's Vineyard by way through the mountains, with photo evidence of the crime! Now to get back for the big races this weekend coming!

Heading north on the road that morning was oppressive, it was so incredibly hot! While following a dump truck full of huge boulders on a causeway, I didn't like the sag of overweight look in the rear tandem wheels on the drivers side. Figuring the heat, the load, and me not wanting to be there behind him, at next available chance I blew by him with a rumble! Seconds later, that frigging back set of tires blew out with the stress, and that truck slammed sideways on the causeway blocking the road. Who the hell knows what would have happened to me! With a little look up to the heavens and a prayer I rode on, finally hitting the mainland. The sunset wasn't far away, coming up through Homestead, what an eerie look up ahead. It looked like a set of thunderhead clouds out over the Atlantic with the sun set putting a hell of a slide show on those clouds! Turn up the satellite radio and speed up buddy!

It wasn't long before it happened again, the *Pipeline* of life happened again so as your conscious could not miss it. Right as I was about to approach the Miami area, there it is, the music, USSR!!! As Ringo started the lyrics 'Flew in from Miami beach BOAA, didn't get to sleep last nite!', oh fuck, I am looking at the highway exit sign for Miami Beach!!! Holy shit, that's definitely my late brother riding with me, on my shoulder, protecting, having fun fucking with me again! "Hey CW", I screamed as I sped up, wild times!! Never ride faster than your angels can fly though. Look at them awesome menacing clouds, wow! Over the next rise, life became a scary reality fast when those wild clouds had just opened a deluge to create a big collision up ahead.

First thing you know, you can't see, cause it's Florida thick tropical downpour, oh my God. Last thing I remember was knowing I needed the breakdown lane to slow with out being smashed and holy shit, it's hard to stay up it's too much water under the tires!!! I was about to let out the primeval scream when from behind me a loudspeaker sounded, "I got your back keep going, keep going, slow down, coming off to the right just a bit more, more, that's it your good, go fifty more yards we are taking a sharp right into a ball field!" It was a Florida State Trooper who rode bikes and understood exactly what was happening and responded perfectly, or I was about to have some trouble. He got out a blanket that we threw over the bike as small hail started. We talked about the trip I was living large, and where I was heading now as I got prepared to head out. Advise as to a short cut to gas and back onto the highway as to not be delayed was great, that trooper was cool! The gas station turned out to be crazy when the Indian guy came out to me with a bat after I got gas I payed him for. He just wasn't wild about me changing some wet shirts and I was about ready to have a scene outta control, when my trooper buddy showed up. He was across the intersection looking at the traffic and couldn't help noticing the guy he just saved getting gas, when the 'shit' started. Again this guy was there, as I finished I asked him to escort me outta Florida it was getting surreal, but with a laugh and a 'shiny side up' he left as I did. I used his trick to miss the shit accident on the highway, it was the balls! On northbound!

Stopping only for the usual gas or mental sanity walk to keep myself fresh, the trip was like clockwork. Listening to that engine at thirty three hundred rpm surely was my favorite sound. Coming into about eleven thirty I was just minutes from the Daytona Beach Exit so I always think of seeing Jr. win there live, and no different tonight. My dream got blown away though, when the boom that interrupted was the sound of a rear tire failure! The car I just had passed was locked up solid as I went from side to side of the highway saving her! It took all preemptive correct guesses on my part, there was no way I could have thought about it, no time! The end result was me going off having to actually use the exit to bring it to a stop on a road surface, instead of off the highway. The guy in the car following that missed me, thank God, was there to help me get off the bike. I had to lean her too far over for the kickstand because of my backrest. Why drop her now right? I called the Daytona Harley shop's 24 hr line and got some great roadside assistance from the service manager on call that night. After having the bike on a lift in the shop safe and sound, and not having any idea where to stay, I opted for the pick nick table outside their diner. I told him the sunrise would wake me. A quick trip up the road for beers and he gave me one of the rooms they have for certain issues that arise, he wanted me to come down out of the sky too. I had a rush going on from the blowout for sure!! That was a fast six pack. When I ate in the diner at Harley the next morning, they said my bill was on the house, I was the lucky shit from Mass.! Really! Everybody knew about the crazy bastard that didn't bash the full dresser with a blowout on the highway! Luckiest guy in town they said! C'mon man don't fucking freak me out again this morning, I had just drank that night away, I thought!

Meeting the service manager again that morning was neat, I thanked him for all the hospitality. He just insisted it was his duty, and the owner started asking if he could buy my bike for the new huge showroom at dealership they were building not too far away. No fucking way I started joking, but he got more serious by the moment. They had a collector series rack about ten feet up in the new showroom and he could not find a Liberty Electra Glide Classic like mine anywhere, nevertheless one so frigging pristine! It was a fun idea, and finally my baby was ready. Their senior tech and I had been already talking a lot because he could not believe no damage to the wheel or anything. Attentive careful inspection, then doing all the fluids. He was getting ready as he left for his quick test drive after the repair. The front wheel locked right up in the shop! He almost dumped it right in front of me! What the fuck?! Two techs in the immediate area came together, she went back up on the lift, let's look at this. He told me, "you stay right here to see this, we did nothing to the front end of this bike!" I know, I know, jeezzz now I was freaking out!

Ten minutes and a great tech taking things apart found the brand new bearings I had just put in before I hit the road in a bunch of pieces, holy fucking shit!!! All the techs were there in a minute to look at the scene and a lot of head shaking was going on. About what? About me being the luckiest guy in the state! If that tire didn't blow, the bearings were probably going to break and fucking launch me at eighty mph into guaranteed death, or at least close to it! After inspection and only that wrong, yeah fix it let's go baby! While all this was going on, the lunch break had them playing my birthday numbers in the afternoon lottery drawing, all the techs were in on it. I was just shitting myself still.

'Luckiest guy in Florida', is that a badge of honor or what, I was thinking. Time to pay the bill. I heard a shitload of screaming and laughing as I went to pay my bill. It was a great one for a tire, fluids, front end repair, the room and breakfast were on the house. So, being as lucky as you are, "what the fuck, you will not believe we just hit the afternoon numbers using your birthday!" "Are you shitting me? And I wasn't in on it? Fuck!", I said. "Relax" he said, "we're putting the bill together now, and we are covering half, this has been a blast!" I was thinking, no matter how fast the bike was the night before, it wasn't faster than my angel!

It felt like leaving a group of friends as I rumbled out of the service department there, those boys kicked in six hundred bucks! Finally, it didn't take long for my trust in angels and my baby were in full force again, finding myself at 84 mph. I got back up to Charlotte and the stories and videos of the trip to Key West had everybody in fucking tears laughing. I brought the broken bearings in a box for people to witness for themselves, every single time getting a gasp, and wow, from anyone knowing about mechanics. I got to enjoy the race crowd of friends and taste the home made ice cream, hand cranked, made special for me that night too, it was awesome. With the racing weekend behind us I was already getting ready for the northern cruise. I have to say the rest of the way home was just awesome that night driving overnight with the moon chasing me across the sky. The cities were blasting by me in my world of roaring speed surrounding me, angels leading the way. It was always awesome to catch the semi trailers and use the wind whipping by them, the ones that rode always gave the wave and lights flash, a lot of them do and the first to help when ya need it too. Through New York and now thinking of all the possibilities at that Conneticut diner, my tape-worm was screaming feed me!

So much to eat I could barely move and back home I headed for the final leg of the journey. Coming back to the area you grow up is always special. I remember every time I got off an overseas flight I would drop to my knees and kiss the earth, America! Some laughed, others get it, I felt the same getting back home from one of my crazy trips I always took. Life was so great, people I met out there were always fun. I had people over the years give me a key to their house and the address telling me I will beat them there on the way home, steaks in the fridge and have a blast. I always found it to be incredible, especially how the southerners are! Brian and Lisa, Kelley and Steve, the Wades from GA., Karen and Ken, Ed from Canada, and the Birmingham connection, thanks for all the fun times and sharing your camp sights and race arguments with me! My 'Angel and Liberty' got me home that time to tell the stories of Riding and Free~Fall!

TINA

DOGS CHANGE YOUR LIFE

We all cried our eyes out together in that garage that night. I was so excited to get back home even if only for a few weeks on leave, but this was the worst news of my life now! No familiar ring of the collar, oh say it isn't so, as I cried my fool head off. It all started as the family moved to the town because of my father's job. He was a boilermaker, one of the trades that built our power plants, he often spit up gross stuff, but then said at least the money was clean! We had moved to bottom floor not far away from our new house across the fields. Glad it was so close that everyday that my brother CW and I would run across the cow field after school to see the guys building the house for our family. One day as we blasted into the house, it was in the plastering phase. You can just imagine kids coming through the house as the guy, smoking a cigarette, spitting on the floor cursing at the kid mixing the plaster to move his fucking ass and, don't forget the special sauce this time! As we came down the hall we came in the room he was plastering and told him this was our house, this actually to be my sister's new room. We got the 'beat it kid!' Oh well, we would just go play in the basement puddles. When we moved in the old man had a touch for the speed in which he could grow a lawn. Neighbors were asking him for the secrets. One used to really want to know how he got the chocolate brown paint on the house so damn shiny too. Not his trade, but for a boilermaker, he could build, grow, or do anything. Great proof was always in the pudding. The far back of the yard got prepared for the summer garden, he could grow stuff too. Tomato plants filled barrels going to anyone who wanted them, green beans, corn, and always green peppers too. A lot of work, he didn't care. I just wanted to be with the old man and I enjoyed it. One night after watering the new lawn, pulling weeds in the massive garden, it was finally dinner time, yea! Mom's favorite pork chop dinner she made so well. I can still smell it in the air just thinking about it! I will say, the usual cleanup was happening really fast tonight. Get in the car kids lets go, we have an errand to run. It seemed so fast, we were back in the town almost where we used to live, only further away this time, new territory for me. This is it, we were at a small house in the middle of nowhere. The lady that came out worked with my mother, and so the introductions began. After a short time, the reason became apparent why we were there. In a small entry way to the house, there they were, a litter of puppies! Wow, there were like five or six of them! Whew, I didn't know if we were there to only to look at them. It was just fun to see the mother with the little puppies. That's when my father told us to pick one out, we were taking one home! There were kittens too and sure enough we got one of them also!! Wow, what a night. I picked out the kitty, and my sister picked the dog. Nice, we were outta there! The cud-dling scene on the way home, the three kids in the backseat with the two animals already sleeping on the ride. However when we got home the dog and cat thing came into being. Screaming at my sister as to how the dog would kill the cat, and her visa versa. When we put them down they did what they do, we closed the door, and saw them in the morning. Opening the door was one of great expectations about what they may have done to each other. There they were, sound asleep against each other in front of the chimney. Tina, was a mutt, a mix of Spaniel and Collie. The cat, Sam was just cool. That cat came like a dog when you called her, and Tina would race her to the door. When you let Tina out to do her business in the morning, she'd first run around the house to the glass door outside to jump around for a bit to just let you know she was there. A race from the front door to the porch, then she was gone. When she returned from the fields behind the yard she usually had a treat she hunted down, be it a rat, squirrel, or rabbit. She would drop it at the glass slider to display for us. I can't believe that most days she actually scored. Tina was a well fed home animal, but would have fared well in the wild for sure. Tina just ran by the bike and everywhere I went. If I was in a neighbors house, my mother knew it driving up the street, because Tina would dig a quick hole by the front step of the house I was in, and lay in it until I left. She was the only dog they'd let into the bowling alley I hung at down the street as a kid. I worked there for free bowling, and all the fun one could muster. I couldn't believe Tina knew all of Route 6 crossing the highway. She knew which way to look and would never run in front of a car. Thinking now, she was smarter than the average bear! We would lay on the grass as kids just looking up into the sky after some baseball catch, or whatever we were playing. That dog would come up, flop over and end up on her back rubbing about near you. She chilled til you got up, or we got called in for supper. I swear she was just imitating us. I could never beat her to the door either. There was a sound that always was a treat to hear. It was always the jingle sound of her ID and license together as she ran, or just when she moved, it was part of her. She would not even come in the house when we called her in, she loved the garage. That was her world, and she shared it well with the cat. I saw her more than once when we had a litter of kittens. Tina watching the kittens in the box, while Sam was out hunting or whatever. There's Tina with a kitty in her mouth putting it back in the box by the scruff of the neck like mama cat! Unbelievable! Funny thing is, she loved being in the neighbors house, she'd be up on the beds and everything! I could never figure it out and never will. As driving age came you would have to make sure she was in the garage.

She'd chase the vehicle I was in, all the way to Rogers spa, a local restaurant and store a few miles away. As a kid if you only knew how much they loved you.

Time ticked by, and summers were spent on the Vineyard working and going crazy, but every weekend it would be Tina time! She was my dog by now it seemed for the most part I guess, of course the families, but mostly mine, that's my take. High school gone, just kicking around working on the Vineyard and couldn't wait to get back home that fall. I didn't see Tina aging because we were no longer on the bike rides with her running full stride aside anymore, so how could I. She still bolted around that house damn good though, she was fast, and fun. You could do anything with that dog, we had her in tree houses too. She scared the shit out of me one day while fishing on the Slades Ferry Bridge. She usually just laid there waiting, this time she jumped! I almost jumped in after her, but thank goodness for common sense, I would have not made it. I was screaming bloody murder, but she just swam back to shore, and came all the way back around up onto the bridge again, Tina, what the hell are you trying to do to me!!!! Holy shit!

I guess the Air Force had a hold on me and I have to tell you, sometimes you don't know if you make the right decisions or not, but I was going. Never forget that eerie morning just before my Christmas birthday when I left. My mother had been crushed since I told her I was going, and my brother was swearing never to talk to me again for breaking up the family band. Mind you I loved it, but I needed to see the world baby! Razor blades on the floor taking off wax, when we heard Merry Christmas fuckers! Ha, I was so worn down already in a few days, I really forgot it was my birthday, boy did I fuck up I thought!

Basic training went by fast, then on to tech school for a few months, then get to go home for leave! Tech school seemed to take forever, I was getting the homesick taste in my mouth. Finally the day came for all the celebration of finally knowing where you were going for duty, me it was Nebraska, but let's get back home. I can't wait to hug my frigging dog! I'm sure she must be missing me by now and I'll hear that jingle when the door opens and sit in the garage for an hour at least with her like every time with her brown eyes just looking up at ya as ya patted her under that white spotted chin!

It was a three jump plane flight, and it couldn't go fast enough for me. I have to tell ya, it was better to see mom happy at the terminal to pick me up. The last time I saw her eyes crying out on the sidewalk as the bus pulled away, with a, 1 4 3, of fingers for I love You, it crushed me for months, actually, life, cause I am weeping about it now writing about it! Things matter! I don't know how they did it, but they held it until I unlocked that door and came in the garage..........NO jingle! Oh NO! They wanted me to concentrate on my mission of Air Force duty and not be upset over something I could not change. I was so mad, I had it explained to me that a few days after I didn't come home she stopped eating. She had to know probably by the vibrations of hurt in my mother's heart and soul, she could feel it. She never really ate again and shortly thereafter had to be put down. The poor broken heart on Tina, they lost her. I sat in the spot by that chimney in the garage where her and I did for her whole life. I was just rocking back and forth for hours uncontrollably weeping, while holding that collar. Just listening to the thing jingle every now and then, it still breaks me! I loved her so very much!

Thirty two years later, I screamed south to get a dog that needed a rescue situation to help her. My mother was on oxygen with a walker, but doing reasonable, so I headed out! When I got to this dog she looked up at me, and wow, she has those same damn eyes, and that color of the nose was exactly the same shade too. When I picked her up and looked closer we were eye to eye, I popped the easy question. Hey pup you have the same eyes I have seen before, do you want 'Tina' for your name?? Two huge licks answered that one, so there it is, let's get in that car and race North dog! All the way home she listened to loud music, and was ready for the party. When we got home the next few years were crazy, chapters for other times. Tina is still with me as I write this, she's been there through some of the toughest times of my life. Actually, she saved me, god bless TINA !!

MAX OR MAUREEN
GROWING UP HAVING FUN

Oh baby, I think the cops may have something to say about this, don't you think? Both of them were laughing and, the answer I was thinking, didn't happen. Uh OH! This could get ugly, your really doing this? Basically it all started months earlier, when a friend got his first car. I guess the days of his parents car use were over. Funny thing is though, it was a stick, and he really didn't drive it well at all yet, yeah yet! Several people used to give me rides to and from from school. Some because of the morning fun, others because they were in one of the bands at school also. The guy who got this car was one hell of a sax player in all the bands. I'd say Steve could play with the best! Our music program at school was intense, we got to do everything! The music director was such an enthusiast he got the town labeled 'Musictown U.S.A.' We had special field show competitions, and parades that still happen today. We're talking seventies when it started. Trips to Washington, New York City, tours with several bands starting way up north in Plattsburgh, New York, slid though Montpelier, Vt, Manchester, NH, then down the highways, south to

Virginia. Trips went to Florida to compete nationally in street and field shows with the marching band, it was awesome.

Part of the percussion section was Alan a year younger, but with talent that would be unmatched by many. Oh yeah I know one better. He was so good that when a group of us were at a Buddy Rich concert one night, Rich while up front with the towel around his shoulders, wiping his brow, glass in the other hand. Makes an announcement, "oh yeah, there's the next ME right there, Jeff, stand up!" Turns out Jeff was a friend of my brother's, whom I would run into several years later. I would get kidnapped by CW to do errands, that's how I would get to know these sickos! All his friends and music buddies were awesome with jokes. Most of the time it would go back and forth for hours.

Some of the bands would practice in sections, that's how Al and I got to be good friends. It was always fun to watch him bust his brother Brian's balls, no matter what they did! The band practices would go late after school depending on which band. Sometimes you'd find yourself back there at six to practice for local plays until eleven. Needless to say, you become great buddies with a few common interests and then, there you go. Al and I did tennis lessons at the local racket club, his family had me in their pool club, that was always fun! His father owed a local tire shop and knew everybody, he hooked us up for driving school when it finally came time and everything. Funny, he'd ask his customers for a cigarette, back then you smoked everywhere you wanted to. They always gave him one, he would put it in his lips and never light it. They always offered to light it too. He told me, ask for something they will give it, all the time, never be afraid to ask kid! He would sell a car a week that he would fluff and duff. Wouldn't you know, they always had new tires, go figure!

I didn't even have my license yet, and yelled at Steve to jump outta that drivers seat. He pulled right over into the bowling alley parking lot. I was going to get a broken neck if he didn't get better with this clutch. Turns out I bet he would have wished he kept that car to this day, she was an awesome Mustang, it was bright red, paint job was still excellent, interior like new. Who ever had it before though had just a bit of work done, it was a heavy clutch I felt. The only reason I would know is my brother in law taught me on his race car. He drove it from Warwick to Somerset, a get gas for each trip kind of car! It was the 'Jade Grenade' with baby moon hub cabs, totally understated but, it would make your eyes open wide! A trip to the store found me in the back seat of it one day, and CW in the passenger seat. A guy at the store yelled at Jack, "you wanna run that fucking rat!??" Uh oh, we pulled out going down toward the power plant down the road. Second gear had the car just chunking along, the cam was big, so that baby was ready. Here he comes. Jack let the guy get by us about fifty feet. Then I found myself pegged against the back seat as we took off like a jet fueled rocket it seemed to me, holy shit! By the time we passed him we were heading onto the highway overpass heading down to the power plant. That guy just got his doors blown off, alright we kicked his ass. I was looking back toward him fading back behind us on the drivers side. Looking back forward was, oh no! A vehicle heading down the point hadn't made up their mind, they were sideways across the street. We'd never make the hard left to Earl's house down the point, and we may crash this asshole trying to make it straight to the power plant. Jack pounded the brakes, the car kinda slid right. The car across the road crept forward just enough for us to blow the fuck by at a speed fast enough, all of us would have been on the cloud with the three stooges after the crazy episode! Yeah the stooges music! "Yeah it'll cost ya a hundred to see the engine looser", Jack yelled to the dude. We went home with the loaf of bread, it had to be crushed, whew!

I tried to slowly show Steve a better idea to get this baby going. We went around the bowling alley lot a few times and, what the hell, who needs a license. I dove around all the time, seems all my friends let me, so did my father. I drove us to school for the night session of band practice, we were doing the Lion King play, it was finally time for the orchestra practices with cast too. I wouldn't have even been there for that, but I ran the lights for the stage, and did all the sound effects. Always a good time, not only that, the chicks dressed fast back stage, ah yes, I got an eyeful more than once. Al would join us for the ride home and that would always be a hoot. Really, you don't think we went straight home. Some nights would find us on the twelve mile drive, Newport. There was a time we were definitely lost in Providence. Yeah we were like country bumpkins in that place. One time Alan had been taking trombone lessons so it was in the trunk, hmm this could get us in trouble! With out thinking another second, there he is testing the slide while sitting in the back seat. The back windows weren't all that big so, yeah, with all windows open, and Al leaning out doing a back and forth full trombone vaudeville slide, that's how Providence saw us that night. I think some of the drunks hanging out that night must still remember it.

The blinkers on that mustang had indicator lights on the hood that shot back toward the driver. The left had the name, 'Max', so naturally whenever a left was needed from then on it seems, no matter who's car we were in, left became ~ Max! I bet we know who that guy was banging, or married to anyway, as kids, we wanted to think, bangin'! Yeah the right banger was, 'Maureen', hence from that point all right turns ~ Maureen, we'd do it without thought. Many fun times in that car, no matter who was driving it, we all did.

Steve still remembers it, because I asked him last year when he bought a car at the dealership. Steve showed up on my day off and Dave sold him a car. Why they show up when your off kills me. Dave was telling me about Steve getting a vehicle, immediately the story came out, how could it not. Sometimes they at work wish I wouldn't tell the stories, but at least I have them. Better yet with all the brain damage, lucky I can still remember them! Later that afternoon, Steve smiled talking about it with that, lucky we made it grin!

I jumped into telling Dave about one of the good ones. The basketball court near Al's house had a tennis court up a little hill about fifty feet away. For some reason, the walk was too far and that Mustang just shot around the lot once, then around the basketball court and headed toward the grass to the tennis court. Boom, when it hit the huge bump, I would call it a hill, Steve hit the roof the car. You could hear it, ouch. Later on that evening after the normal burger joint run, we were riding around town looking for things to get into. We stopped at a local drug store for drinks. When we came out there was a grocery cart there. The next scene had us tying it to the bumper of Steve's car. Are you shitting me, the cops will have something to say about this one! My old man said if the cops ever called the house holding me, he was going to tell them, keep me! You guys are crazy! At this point we were kind of deciding who was riding in it. Didn't take long for Alan to grab the trombone out from the trunk and declare he was the rider! Steve fired up that car and semi bucked his way out of the lot heading toward Buffington St. It was a turn to the right, and up the hill we went. With Al in tow, not too fast we headed up the hill. The whole time he was doing his famous vaudeville slide. This time though we weren't in some crazy city! It's quiet around eight thirty on a weeknight in Somerset!

One of the girls in the marching band lived up the street here, oh yeah, they're getting a concert! Their front living room door at that house was always open, so the storm door would let us do the deal. The car slowed way down chugging along in first gear, Al was doing the very best vaudeville slide he could. That brought Sue's mom to the door. Within seconds they were all at the door with thumbs up! They knew we just weren't right! Just about a half mile up the road, oh yeah, oh fuck, here we go. A police cruiser coming the other way. He gave the blue light flash, laughing, as Al blasted him with the 'slide'! When by us he wanted to show us, he gave us the siren and kept going! "I can't fucking believe he didn't just arrest us", I screamed to Steve and Alan as we were leaving the shopping carriage in the church parking lot. I remember jokes about it having to be the end of his shift and he doesn't want to do the paperwork. We just slid home so that cop would not see that car cruising the rest of the night. I lost touch with Al when years later he became a ski enthusiast, and moved to the mountains. Nice to see though that 'Max and Maureen' were still in Steve's memory bank.

KEEP 'EM

SURVIVING MY COUSIN

"Son of a whore!" Well I have to tell you, I know he had just cracked his hand so hard it wasn't funny, but my cousin Kev and I just pissed ourselves laughing. His father Kicker, had just cracked himself really good. I never could remember what he was even working on under that hood that day, or even which car for that matter of fact. The only thing I know is, that was the first time I heard that one. We were laughing so hard, really, I think I pissed myself. Kicker gave us a laugh with that one liner, that would last a frigging lifetime. Still forty eight or so years later I do. It was a loud scream, it just had that Maine drawl on it that made it, well, funny! Kicker was the kind of guy that would go for a ride in a blizzard, they'd always stop and grab us too. We'd end up in Connecticut to one of our aunt's houses. Yeah in a blizzard, we loved surprising people. All the adults would be playing cards, which left Kev and I up to no good. Not all the time, but most. Kicker would bail you out it seemed with all kinds of things. He could fix anything. He got calls to tow cars out of marshes, oh yeah it was stuck! I must say never a grouch, and always a side of the mouth smile. The other side reserved for his favorite cigar, lit or not.

It was great time to create a reason to have to stay down their house during the summer sometimes, after all, there were summer girls there! We had a hoot of a time swimming in Nanaquaket Pond, every now and then water skiing, and fishing. One of the dumber things was jumping off the bridge near the seafood place. Holy shit, are you sure there are no pylons in there? Youth doesn't think much, splash! I remember my balls getting crushed by my pants wanting to blow up hitting the water. We were talking the girls into jumping, in true hopes no bathing suit would be on them when they surfaced! Always thinking! Summer concerts at North Park in Fall River gave us a chance to get in some great stuff, again, fun times. I still frigging have no idea what bands ever played. I was too busy chasing the summer girls around. The mini bike rental place in Westport got it's fair share of abuse too. I think I must have hurt several trees there. Things always got fucked up when we went there. Of course chasing each other, trying to touch the other guy's back tire while sliding around trees on those trails may have not have been smart. Oh well, I can't even remember if that was a cause of one the many concussions!

Leaving that last paragraph may remind me. First, there was a Chevy we roughed up and painted with spray cans, Ford blue no less. Lorraine, his mom made the second trip to a different store, so we could get the other eight cans. What the hell do all the body shops charge so much for a paint job, when cuz and I did it in a day, outside at the house! We thought it was awesome. After years now of working in the car industry, I realize, we fucking massacred that car! My fucking word what a blast we had! That is the Sepowet Point, yeah I need to be pulled out car! Kicker never really said a thing, just that grin while chewing the cigar. Many miles just having fun were logged in that car, we went anywhere we could.

Best thing about your crazy cuz picking you up to go to a coffee house I used to run on Friday nights is, well, everything! The freedom of being able to get around with out much parental restriction gave you some latitude to pull stuff, before and after the hours the coffee house ran. That had us written all over it! Kev and I would be on the run. One time after dropping someone off, I got out and ran around the car. No one else did. When I heard the car go in gear, oh no cuz, you fucking ain't getting out of here and leaving me! I jumped on the hood like Manix! Problem is, the fucking actors always did a, 'CUT', then they put a stand in there. Then, did the fucking stunt. Not me, I was holding on as he went from side to side, accelerating. I know I must have at least *looked* like Manix with my legs sliding from one side of the hood to the other. Holy shit, what a ride. The whole time all of us laughing like hyenas. I can't remember to the day who was in the front seat besides Kev. I am lucky actually I remember a fucking thing anyway! Finally, all things that accelerate have to do a bit of 'stoppage' at the end of the street. Exactly is what that fucking cousin of mine did! A bunch of backward rolls, and I think there was a pine tree involved! I just remember that night limping into the house. I went to shower, and right to bed. I think I had to score one of those big 'Cs' for concussion there. For days I was throwing up and having a hard time walking around school. I felt better in time for Friday though, when coffee house time happened again.

The Mustang pulled in the driveway, get in let's go. Here we were heading to NH to have cuz race grudge night. It's kind of just a fun event, since when can a regular souped up car beat a dragster! The ride up there was fun with the hum of that crazy car. Upon getting there he signed in got the appropriate numbers on his car and we were ready, well almost. Expose them headers and let that thing rumble! Kev had fun watching dragsters coming up on him and blasting by. Myself, I wouldn't want to be in front of 'em. Riding home we were telling jokes, and humming along until Route 79 North Fall River. Boom, oh well. That bastard got worked on for a day in the street here until she drove away.

The next Friday we were painting the coffee house and blasted out of there early. Well not until, I painted one girl's tongue that stuck it out at me. A full brush of green paint in my hand, to this day, I swear, it wasn't planned, it was just a reaction! Another one kind of needed some cooling down, so I co2 fire extinguished her! My fucking word, I'm lucky I didn't get my ass kicked by them two that day. You can already tell some stuff was about to go on. As Kev took a left out of the church lot, we went down the hill, but in short order ended up on a side street stealing some massive frigging pumpkins. After a quick getaway, pealing out and all, we were on the road. Oh yeah, get out the bat. Bat? Let's take out some mailboxes, well that sounded like fun. What chooches, but we were gonna have some fun. Next scene, I was hanging out the passenger side as he drove with no oncoming traffic, popping a few mail boxes. A few boxes with shitty install, flew past the hood of the car and we almost hit them. Fun times!

A few roads later, we were traveling on a major cut through road in my town. Right after the town line coming back into Somerset I was cracking a mailbox, the guy who owed the property at that repair shop flipped out when he saw me! Holy shit, he's in a truck chasing us! I jumped in the back seat and used one of those pumpkins on a curve to the right to take him out! It rolled perfectly across a lawn then back into the front end of his truck. By that time we were already heading back at him, and blew by! Screwing up the road we had 'pumpkin' man beat. Problem is, we took a right on the wrong street. Instead of being on the escape route, we were down a dead end street. Trapped like rats, rats I tell ya! It's surprising how long an hour is when you don't want to be somewhere. Not much was discussed, other than whether the cops where going be involved or not. Patience did not prevail, we started the car and headed down the road with no headlights, it seemed clear. As soon as the headlights went on, so did all the blue lights heading toward us! Hum, wondering how this will go over on the home front. The Swansea P.D. didn't want two kids with a *pumpkin* rap! The Somerset cop, an asshole, made Swansea take us in, oh boy! Now, I'm fucked.

Thank god they never found out about all the mailboxes. It's just that 'fuck' didn't have a sense of humor. I mean, come on two teenagers, a bat, and a car? What could possibly go wrong? I will never forget the cops asking our home phone numbers. I told them not to bother calling my father, I was gonna end up living here! They wanted it anyway, my brother answered the phone, said, "they're not home." He hung up and blew off the cops. Kev and I knew they were at his house playing cards, after divulging the information, the cops called there. You could hear the speaker phone in the cop station as the phone rang. Kicker answered the phone, a low key "h'low". A brief conversation about who was calling, and Kev's father didn't sound like he fucking cared we were in the hoosegow! Matter of fact he said, "hey Con listen to this." He handed the phone to my father. That same brief explanation from the cop got an interesting answer, but I was told it would happen really young in life. It was, "fucking Keep 'Em!" Then he hung up! The cops laughed their asses off. They called them back later I guess when we couldn't hear them, Kicker and my old man came and got us. I never heard a word about it again. 'Keep 'Em' rang in my mind for years. Needless to say when other shit happened, I called old girlfriends, or my great friend Kathy. She was always up to helping me get my car and get out of jail after a caper!

Life happens, cuz had a great wife and family, he went into the trade of our old men, retired too. Surprised he made it too, being the fucking prankster he is. I'm shocked one of the older boilermakers didn't weld him in some crawlspace, never to be found again. Missed are the days of our youth, smashing and crashing around the greater area, but always having fun and nobody, well I don't know about that, ask my back, got hurt. Tell ya, I'm surprised we survived ice skating across giant sheets of ice that broke off in the fresh and salt water mixed pond. The puck ran out there, and as you skated it all broke behind ya, just jump to the next sheet! We had to be out of our fucking minds! What a way to die, but, again, never even crossed our minds, just skate faster screw that puck!! I'll never forget my cousin's dog Lucky, she looked like Tina, almost like from the same litter. Then as the life bubble expands so far it blows up. Some time you just have to realize it was just age, we didn't give up. Decades flew by. One day on social media he befriended me, ha, a friend? No it's my cousin! We reminisced and laughed at what the old man said that night, "just fuckin' Keep 'Em!" Ha!

LET ME DRIVE
COMING BACK HOME

Holy shit you almost just killed me with fear and now you what?
My hands were still shaking, I should say vibrating, and my fingers
tingling! I had just hit the steering stick in the biplane I was riding
in. On a motorcycle journey to Key West from Martha's Vineyard I
took an unfortunate fall at the motel the night before. I came crashing down while leaving the room on the way out to see the sunset at
the motel beach, and mind you, miraculously without spilling not
one frigging drop out of that Heineken I had just opened! In the
crowd enjoying the sunset included a girl that worked for a local
chiropractor, and I needed one for sure, I had a minimum of two
weeks left of riding on this trip. It was awesome, first thing the next
morning I pulled up to the crazy looking flamingo pink building,
it had an articulating sign with back snapping jokes. Best part is,
he turned me onto this guy I was flying with right this second, oh
fuck, what a scary fucking fun ride this is! So after a bunch of deep
breaths and purposely talking myself into a calmer state, I grabbed
the stick to steer this awesome bird. Sweetie Pie was her name, all
painted beautifully in a shiny coat of a radiant blue, oh yeah, she

was gorgeous. I didn't find out later this was the sixth rebuild. What 'da fuck did you just say? The sixth, holy shit I didn't know that til we crab landed later. "Now just head it to that light house straight ahead, doing good." That's was Jim's voice in my headset giving me all the instructions to bring us back to the runway. Notably as I took over the altitude got higher ever so slightly. That led to all the Harley riding getting high joke laughter, gotta love it!

What a nice drive it was though to fly that majestic aircraft, similar to the one Howard Hughes owned. A Waco Bi Plane, it's engine a deep sounding monster! I was excited to have the experience. It seemed like all the time in life, I either wanted to drive it, or someone else wanted me to. That leads me to the earliest driving experience I could remember, with this smacked up brain! My brother and sister had this awesome pedal machine in the shape of a jet. Oh yeah, to a baby like me at the time it was huge. Every time they drove it on the street, they used a mild incline on the street to just enjoy a glide. I wanted to drive that baby. Kept getting grabbed out of it in the yard by my bro, tossed aside, as they went out on the street and got crazy with it for a while. I would hang at the small evergreen trees street side the old man had planted. Four of them evenly spaced a few feet set back from the street, yeah they were as tall as me. My mother was making sure the older kids didn't fuck me up! I mean not for nothin', but she caught my brother CW, caught him right in the act. Years ago he was leaning into the carriage I was napping in. With a squirt gun, you know what was going on!!! Yeah right in the face! His excuse when my mother came flying out and grabbed the thing from him was, "oh the neighbor was burning and he had ashes on his face mom!" He was a three stooges enthusiast, which would dog me my whole life with him! Quickly she was jumping up and down on the damn squirt gun until it was in pieces! It must have been quite a sight, I heard the story a million times, even from other relatives.

I guess there must have not been any other kids around that day. My brother decided to direct his attention to me to play. This might not be good, but how would I know, I was too young to have learned, yet! Hey, there we are messing around with the jet, yeah baby, I love this damn thing, what a wing span. It even had all the markings that a top notch Air Force fighter pilot would be proud to be sporting. For sure, she was damn awesome! Just get in, get in. My bro just basically smashed me in the thing and here we go. No I wasn't even steering, didn't know how, but we were on the way out to the street. He shoved the jet along grabbing the steering set and jostling it into place on the street at the top of, as a kid, looked like a mountain. Next, CW gave it the shove! Whew, for two seconds, that was fun. All I saw was a face full of bushes from the house across the street, as I crashed them but good. Yup, the crying and all, it was my last drive with the jet. Fuck it though, the jets to take a jump seat in the real Air Force years later, made that memory disappear. Naw, they definitely couldn't let me drive!

Two Chevy's ended in the driveway, his and hers, a memory to behold, the picture of me sitting on the hood at six years old. Their license plates just one number apart as they were bought at the same time that night. Coming to think about it now, many years later after working in the car biz, you never forget as a salesman, a two car deal! The Impala being dad's was definitely the one I liked, and wouldn't you know, the first I got to drive. Oh maybe on the way home from Horseneck Beach or some restaurant, yup, on the lap and steer this bastard! I always thought I did great at it. I just know I washed the paint off both of those fucking cars, so I could back them out to the street to turn them around to rinse them. Yeah the hose reached, I think they liked to just amuse me, and I was driving them, yeah baby!

As I got closer to driving age, I worked late down at the bowling alley. The old man decided to let me take his car to the alley, it's a half mile away, what could possibly go wrong!! The theory being I would not be walking home so late. Go slow and be careful, you know how to. I don't know what gets into kids, but in no time after mopping some lanes and disinfecting bowling shoes, I wanted a pizza! Yeah and I will go get it, delivery wasn't what it is today. The next scene, as I was coming back from the pizza shop across town. I spotted my mother's wide eyes looking at me in the traffic driving in the other direction. Never ever remember seeing the car, just her fucking wide open, 'I will kick that kid's ass eyes!!!!' I tried to pretend I didn't even know what they were talking about, but the old man had felt the hood on the car that was, should we say, hot. Yup I was screwed, the keys got handed over and that fun was over, walking again.

That didn't stop me, my neighbor had a Dodge with the buttons to put the car into drive, and a slider I think that put 'er into park. That was the next adventure car. He gave me a lot of rides to school and ran a local coffee house. He would later on groom me to take that place over, when he graduated and left town. Another of the school rides was the buddy with a Mustang that was a stick, I helped the dude with that one, and I got to drive that bitch everywhere. Two wheels became involved at the trails learning that, holy shit, even on dirt it hurts to fucking fall. Are the handle bars straight, nope, pull this way, yup that's good, get back on! Couldn't wait to get a street bike!

License time came and in our family the kids would get given a first car, usually a parental hand down, or they'd find one. Uh oh, I have one already guys. What?....A van. They both gave me the look like it wasn't a great idea. I must have been a great salesman that day, the next scene had a friend of the family going to look at that van. Later in the driveway at home she looked great. She was a sixty six metallic dark brown GMC window van, oh yeah, so nice. Hours later there were curtains made for the windows, mom being a seamstress didn't hurt in all these times. She kept asking the real reason I wanted the curtain that pulled across behind the drivers and front seats, she pretended for me not to know why. The old man and her must have laughed their asses off knowing what plans I had in my mind. She shifted three on the column, just like the car Pat and Jack let me use on the Island during that first summer I stayed with them that I could drive. I would use one of my parent's cars to pick up girls. No father would let a daughter go out with a 'guy in a van', if they only knew!! That curtain would be pulled in the driveway before using the car to go drop them off. My parents were co conspirators I guess now looking back at it, hahahaha!

The summers would find me staying places, I had a great home life. I think I was just a nomad or something. A person from the town not far from us worked with mom, and they had a boat. Oh that was a frigging fun summer, driving is a special word to me when it's in a boat, ahhh. We went fishing, every day, and water skied pending on the tide daily too. I became quite the driver, while the kids father watched his kid ski, just not so close to them rocks right there kid! I drove that damn boat one day, off Plymouth, when we got besieged by a fast moving storm. I guess five trash barrels of Mackerel and three people in an eighteen footer in following storm seas don't mix? I think not! We were getting swamped and the water rushing over the transom had Bill the old man freaked out! Young Billy didn't give a fuck, he was the kind of kid that held lit M-80s! To say the least, I think Billy was whacked, the fucking craziest kid I ever knew. Oh later, he became an instructor for the 82nd Airborne, yeah he was something! Bill put me behind the wheel as he took action to prevent us from having a rather impossible swim to the jetty, way too far away, we weren't gonna make that, it's way too far. I was so happy to see four of those barrels get the heave ho, so we were able to make it back. Billy laughed like a fuck the whole time, like I said, he'd take a blue crab and let it grab his ear to see who would give up first! No, I would not try this at home kids!

The van went by the wayside as I grabbed a Chevy from my dad. First thing you do to get that ride right is to have Nick put a nice paint job on that bitch, with new wheels. Here I go, out to Nebraska. You can't believe what a long ride that is, fucking boring!! I will respect the national truckers after that drive! Boring was the word. That was, until Cleveland! The engine fucked up, still driving, but not fast. I limped into a truck stop and the mechanic found the problem after a half hour. Listen, I was a fucking young kid, who the hell knows if he doinked me or not. As promised, the next morning the thing ran great. It was one hundred and thirty out of the three hundred I had, but she ran again. Omaha or bust, here we go! After a lot more boring fields, and fields, the city of Omaha came into view. The new chapter of life was gonna begin, for real! Strategic Air Command, U.S.A.F., here we go baby, this is where it all runs from! What a drive this was!

Air Force stories for later, but on a personal note, barracks life is really different. Great friends were made that worked in my career field. No I'm not telling you, I'll have to kill you, I want you to read this. Joe turned out to be a room mate along the way. A son of a rancher from Oklahoma, spent a lot of time in Alaska living with his sister. He worked on motors that make the oil run in the pipeline, always interesting to hear stories of that place. Days and nights that last forever, all the serenity. He had great explanations of why people go to hide there. I'm thinking he did, I never was able to find him again in later years. Great artist he was also. One time while we were half buzzed and playing albums for hours of bands I was learning about. Joe drew this nice multi panel picture of a pond we'd ride the bikes to at every chance. While it was always about the drive, we'd enjoy lake 'Zoomie', as we named it, every chance we could. I failed to grab a picture of that, but every one including the commander had made comments about it. I got to talk to him because I had illegal cooking devices in the room, we were not allowed to paint the walls and, glad he never found other things! That would have been a way to end up buffing floors for my service career!

The bike I had was a pea compared to the bigger ones everybody else had, but they didn't mind hanging and not blasting off on me. One such Tennessean from Knoxville, Whit, became a brother in arms, and great friend. We partied our asses off, too many hours of work, and not enough life, that's what we thought. He had a nice bike, a seven fifty four K, oh baby and a nice furring too, man did that thing screw when he nailed it. I screwed my peashooter up trying a wheelie one day. That made me get a bigger bike, oh yeah, that furring too because June bugs were chest bruisers in Nebraska. Now we could ride, yeah the drive to lake Zoomie! On a day off, hitting the highways in any direction was the rule, yeah, no rules that's right. The mid west is so frigging flat, miles away you could see the thunderstorms. Summer in that region and late spring are intense, so we'd flank the storms by hitting a highway to detour us. We'd watch storms go by and sometimes, get in back of them and follow them back to the base. A drive! Last year, forty plus years later, I found Whit on social media. When a picture of the closet door of Joe's painting of lake Zoomie came on my phone, I was catatonic..... stuck in the memory!!!!

I signed up for a special program and I was leaving to go into the Rapid Deployment Forces. It was time to say bye to the boys. My dad had flown in a few days before, so we took him to some of the restaurants we loved. Stella's, home of the best, biggest burgers in the whole world. Yeah, if you eat it all, you eat free place. Holy shit it was awesome. Another, was a place they made their own spaghetti in front of you in an old mill. My old man loved it all. The guys treated my dad like he was theirs. I'll never forget that. The trailer behind the seventy four Celica GT got loaded. There was a motorcycle, couch, stereo system with end table speakers, and lot of clothes. Knowing what I know now, oh yeah, fucking overloaded asshole! Time to leave, I can't believe I'm gonna miss you fucking lugheads!...Damn! ..... Really....! The hugs were done, dad and I hit the road on that drive that would change my life again, forever!

Driving until night was about to set in, we looked for places to get a room, figuring to rest the car. While pumping gas back then they weren't so hard about shutting cars off, we never turned it off. We'd just switch drivers, and a few times took trips on advised directions of gas station guys where a room may be found. Not in the month of August while on the highway back then folks. Pressing on became the mission, even if we go straight home, fuck it we were all in! That drive, it'll always be in my mind. Dad told me stories of how they busted balls on guys at work, the boilermakers were brutal to each other. I heard of stories in the service I had never heard growing up, or ever from him before. Huh, so that's how that Jap rifle ended up in your possession. Yup it was him or me. Thinking to myself, fuuuuuck! Stories were awesome, miles clicking in dawn's light, we were almost to Massachusetts. Never, ever, can you go 'home' again.

Coming closer to the area, it already smelled so different. The ocean scents the atmosphere as your getting closer, oh yeah it's smelling like home. Driving over the Brightman St bridge you could see the differences already. Businesses had moved, a highway interchange near the river, totally different waterfront of Fall River. Wow, it all happened in those few years? It's never the same, the old man said, it'll never be the same Gerry, and he was the only one from the family called me that. Before the service it was Jay. Period. Except for dad, he always called me Gerry. Yeah that last fifteen miles he told me not to be too expectant of the friendships that were before. Life changes and so do people buddy. Driving up our street, my stint of the last two hours of the journey that took twenty six, looking for rooms and detours. Oh my fucking word, it never looked so good to me! Hey mom! Let's back it in, and unload. Being too tired, I crashed into bed until the next day! Trying to start the car the next day, it jumped timing, and screwed up right in the driveway. Turns out, the day before we left, Joe tuned her up at the base garage. He forgot to tighten the nut on the distributor. Holy shit and we made the drive, we had never shut her off!!

On that drive, the old man was so smart. He told me his past, and how the future goes. He told me to always, stay on your toes. He said to beware all of those that you meet. But most of all, don't forget about people in life who make *your* life so special, and neat. He told me how I'd remember the guys I'd just left. He'd never know, because I never told him. On that drive, dad, you hit that fucking nail right on the head!! You never know if it's 'that' drive, that will change your life! Thanks Dad!

I'LL TAKE A BOX
EXPLOSIONS FOR AGES

Holy shit! I went to the left and they were whizzing by! Even when I ran a few bowling lanes away, zip, swoosh, another one flew by, barely missing me. Then I heard the microphone on the paging system click on. An eerie low voice came on. He screamed for me to dance! I looked toward the main desk and there they were, about twenty five or more bottle rockets laying there in a row. Yes, they were aimed out at me on the alleys while I was mopping the lanes. Kevin had them perfectly spaced. When one flew off it never bothered the next. He went down the line with his lit cigarette just firing one off after the other. He only made slight corrections toward the direction I was trying to escape. When it was all over we were laughing, but several times I really thought I would be blasted. Needless to say, that was a fun cleanup that night. The bowling alley was right down the road from my house, so it was a fun, easy job with plenty of free bowling too. Some of the people that worked there became lifelong friends, one was like a second mom to me. Her husband was a mechanic there too, it was always fun to help him repair the pin reset machines. They were old, but with a lot of tender loving care, all forty worked fine thanks to Howe. One day while working on lane twenty four, he pulled out a burnt bottle rocket from under the carpet that rolled the pins. We looked at each other, first thing out of my mouth was, "what's that?" If you don't know what it is, it couldn't be you, that's what I was thinking as a great excuse. Again one late evening right after closing I was mopping the lanes. I heard the microphone click again. I looked and didn't see Kev. The next thing I remember seeing was something hissing in the middle of the lane near me. Uh oh, that doesn't look like something I have seen before. It's definitely bigger than a firecracker for sure. I quickly gave it a little kick into the gutter. The explosion was, oh my fucking word to say the least, incredible! I had already vacated the area like a cockroach when the lights go on! When I looked back though, it was amazing. Blue smoke filled the whole bowling alley. Oh, the best part, a fucking hole in the gutter!! At least six inches blown out! The next scene had us with all the damn doors open. We were hoping no one driving by, like a cop, would think the place was on fire. You could not believe the smoke! Sill laughing, we searched out the piece of gutter to make the fix. The finished job gave us away as the paint didn't match, but it was close. Asked If we knew anything about that the next day by the manager got some funny reaction. Kev and I acted like we didn't even understand the question, and denied the mismatched paint. Needless to say that was my first experience with an M-80.

A few weeks later the conversation about gutter explosion came up. Kev grabbed them from his car and that's when I read the box. It clearly labeled them dangerous and for agricultural use only. I pointed out to my buddy, it said nowhere about blowing up gutters! "Wait" he said, "tonight another caper is happening." Inquisitive and figuring I had nine lives, I was always in. An M-80 and a roll of masking tape will do this one. We spent some time taking masking tape in long lengths ripped in half and wrapped the M-80 into a small hard ball. Just the end of the wick still visible for lighting. A group of cars that hung down in the lower parking lot was going to be the target of this one. Kev held the door open and he had the lighter. I said, "Don't let that fucking thing blow my fingers off, tell me the first sign you see a spark cause I'm chicken and whipping it!" He clicked that lighter and in seconds he screamed, "throw it!" One toss hit on the bottom set of stairs and bounced the thing down rolling into the lot. It made it all the way to the bunch of cars hanging there. When it blew, it managed to be perfectly under one of the cars in the center as they were parked looking out toward the river. Yeah it was just as loud as when inside the building. Maybe because of the compression wrap we added. I remember though how fast every car there started and pealed out leaving the lot! Awesome! On the roof was interesting too. No not the alleys, but United Records next door. It was a huge metal building so the experiment began. As the last customers car pulled out of the lot, we were out, and ready to go. Light the damn thing! He did, and I threw it. Yup right up on that roof. Whoom! I guess there was an overnight security guard in that place. The police were tapping at our doors a few minutes later. When we answered the door we told him we almost called because we just heard a loud bang. That satisfied them and they were gone. We did do another one a half hour later. This time the cops came in and looked around though to find nothing. We got outta there with some nervous laughter that nite.

It's amazing how bored you get fishing off the Brightman Street Bridge at three thirty in the morning when you haven't had a bite yet. Frustration abounded and another one showed up in the tackle box. Was it a beer? No, we had already drank them all by that time. Bait? No, fool, an M-80! Here we go. Just one lit and dropped off that bridge at that time of the morning! Wow!! You could hear echos off the Coca Cola building first. As the sound wave went exponentially further the reverberation under bridge was awesome. The splash was huge, it had to come up six feet. Big Mamie, and the Braga Bridge, gave a great repeat echo too as the sirens started. The city cops just drove over the bridge back and forth and just waived. Somerset however on the second return pass put two and two together. What are the fucking odds, the same cop on shift for the last bangs and booms in the area. "Hey didn't I talk to you two last week at the bowling alley the night with the explosions over there?" Playing 'mickey the dunce' wasn't going over on this cop. Yeah that was wild hey? Just heard another one tonight. Wow it was loud too we said as he got out of the cruiser. What a rush, now I was wondering if Kev had another M-80 in the tackle box, that could be bad. Instead the cop looked over the rail and asked, "if ya even caught a fish, would it stay on the line?" We nervously said we had never caught one yet and laughed. He was onto us! When he dropped me off that night I told Kev, "I'll take a box!"

I don't think two dozen of anything, has given me that much fun in my life! We were about find out what a bowling ball would be like with an M-80 taped in the thumb hole rolling in the parking lot. I took the time it took to tape the thing in just right to leave enough wick to light again. We were getting good at these pranks. Shortly after our last guest left the establishment that evening we went into full fun mode again! At first we didn't know exactly where to do this. We knew for sure after last time with the smoke and everything, it sure as a fuck wasn't going to be inside. Hey the side door, that way we can hear it. In no time we were at the side door with it open at the top of the four stairs. One lite and one kick! Clunk, whoop, clunk, hurry up close the door! Bah-boom!!! The shrapnel from the sixteen pound bowling ball pelted the building. A few seconds later you could hear shit hitting the fucking roof. Holy Shit! We always wanted to be the first witness to our mayhem. Out the door we went. It was a scene to behold. The average size of the pieces was minimum at best. I did run out to grab a few of the bigger pieces that would identify this thing as an exploded bowling ball. Our cop buddy was definitely going to show up! We better get busy acting like cleaning this building! The vacuum cleaner was running and I was not looking toward the door on purpose as our frequent eleven thirty friend showed up. I ignored the tapping on the door glass as if I were Helen Keller on the vacuum. He used his flashlight all around me routine cops know to grab attention. I ran to the door to find out what he was here for. He knew I knew! Pieces of the bowling ball had hit the back of the Somerset taxi building on route 103. The taxi place was located about a hundred yards past the end of our side lot, fifty feet up a slight grassy hill. He had to respond cause they called him. He told us if they hadn't called he wasn't coming, he knew the cause.

Years later the box paid off again. This time I had to be really quiet as I slid up the bathroom window. The only question I had for myself was if I threw this damn thing and it hit the window and bounced back into the house how fucked I'd be. I couldn't contemplate long because Sean was skimming the pool facing the other direction. The dog was in the house so I had to make sure this goes out this window. Oh boy! Nice part is that Sean was walking the top walls of an on the ground pool. He had great balance and was doing a great job until. Boom!! Westport, were we lived was rather quiet. That blast echoed off the neighbor's house and the treeline behind us too. It made a slight digger in the back lawn where it landed too. When I looked out the window to see the carnage it was excellent! Looking through the cloud of blue smoke just let me see Sean drop the skimmer. He went off balance with the big arm wave as he splashed into the pool. "What 'da fuck!?!" he said. Oh it was one of the best to this day. I got his brother one day again, same plan, same result!

One New Years Eve while driving around Providence lost in a friend's car I let a few fly out the window. We were curious to see how loud they'd be in the city. It had great effect, we definitely pissed off a few girls walking on college hill that night! I just rumbled my buddy's brain one night in the service department at the dealer I worked for. Service was open til eleven so as I was leaving on that nice summer night I drove my Reatta right though the service drive check in. I just kept driving as I dropped that bitch behind his podium. I had done it before, but never dropped explosives!! I wasn't allowed to drive through there ever again, I wonder why? A drunken evening found a buddy lighting one I had taped to an arrow broad head tip. I let that bitch fly up in the air behind the house. Balance was an issue for the arrow as it wobbled like crazy and just tumbled. On it's way down it was among the high tension power lines when she blew! Oh for fucking sure I thought I would be in jail that night if it had blown one of those lines down. Nothing though but a neighbor scared shit! "What the hell was that", he screamed.

I happened to be selling a car to a friend of Kev's he brought in a few months back. We couldn't help the stories of M-80's flying around the showroom that afternoon. People couldn't believe the craziness. Oh fucking yes they could, I was involved! I'll never forget that day I told Kev, "I'll take a Box!" Those damn M-80's gave me a lot of fun! I can't believe I managed to actually keep my fucking fingers!!!

THE BRAGA

FROM THE BEGINNING

Don't jump! What the hell is wrong with you? I remember my brother screaming that at me. I was leaning over the edge. We were on the roof of the new house looking at the scenery toward Fall River. It was a summer day in June '65' and I have no frigging idea where my mother had gone. She must have gone shopping, or on an errand. The first thing I knew my brother had the ladder out, and we were headed to the roof of the new ranch house. It took no time for two kids under the age of fourteen to jib up that ladder onto the roof. It was awesome! What a view! To the left you could see parts of the Brightman St. Bridge with North Fall River in the background. Turning slight right we could see the Slades Ferry Bridge heading straight toward the city. The Slades Ferry Bridge was used for the railroad and even horse drawn buggy traffic in the old days. It had a total metal grated one by four inch holed vehicle deck. When in a car crossing it you could look right down to the water, it was scary! The fun thing as a kid would be when it opened with your car stuck on it. The wait would be ten minutes for them to hoist the center span vertical so the tankers with coal or oil could get up river. The bridge had a great aura to it. The tankers with the mass and girth motoring by made the bridge vibrate until they were far enough for them to do the same dance at the Brightman Bridge. The Slades was just wide enough that two cars of the sixties, seventies era could clear each other going opposite directions by the width of a door handle. Hey a miss was as good as a mile. That is what the old man always said anyway. There was a reason to go on the roof that day. CW and I were doing a test run for an observation point for the battleship Mamie being brought to Fall River that weekend. At supper that night we told the old man about being on the roof. I couldn't believe he didn't fucking care! I thought for sure our asses were fried! He worked hundreds of feet in the air, that wasn't anything to him. My mother freaked the fuck out, you could tell by her wide open eyes.

The weekend came to find us all up there on that roof. It was a sunny day, beautiful and clear. You could see the new Braga Bridge in the distance to the right looking at the city. It was still under construction but almost ready to open. Fall River was bringing the Battleship Massachusetts to the city waterfront to be stored for it's retirement eternity. Her nickname was 'The Big Mamie'. She was so tall the top mast had to be taken off to get under the bridge even at low tide. It was a majestic display of American might coming to the city. It was a hell of a sight to behold that day watching the many tug boats pushing hard to move the mighty war ship into place. Only a few days later the top radar towers on the massive ship were erected again to have her in full display. It would not be until the next spring before the two and a half mile Braga bridge was ready for traffic. They decided before it opened to let the public walk it and see the grand spectacle. Oh boy I have to tell ya, it was great. Dad drove the Impala toward the new highway entrance ramp from Somerset and the traffic was heading onto the new bridge.

Police were having a blast telling people as they were parking, "there will be no diving from the bridge!" Everyone was in their in best Sunday clothes as it was Easter '66'. It took quite a while to reach the top highest point of the center span being a mile and a half walk to that point. All the neighbors and people my parents knew were there being such a huge event! Above is a picture of that day. This picture is behind a wall switch plate in my kitchen still today, memories! The scenery from the top center guardrail was incredible. You could see Providence, all of the Narragansett Bay to Portsmouth. The view down though was scary, it was a hundred feet at least. Back then there were no fences there either. That was a day etched in memory. This bridge turns out to be involved in many events of my life, come take this journey.

At twelve years old a friend and I decided a great idea was to jump up onto the catwalk that went from one side to the other under the bridge. It was fun as we scuttled toward the city rising in elevation from the water all the while. By the sixth or so pylon that we were passing over, below us the height was scaring the shit outta me.

When we got to the top we finally sat down for a rest and to observe the spectacular view. I could not believe this fucking thing is moving! Cars would give a bit of a vibration but the tractor trailers made the fucking thing shake!! We were deciding whether to go all the way to the city when the decision was made for us. Coming from the direction of Fall River was two hard looking dudes that looked like they might live up here. If there was to be anything shot at me it would have hit me in the ass, cause I was running full speed. Full speed for the three quarter humped over position you had to be in to navigate the catwalk. I only touched three rungs coming down the ladder off that thing to run the hell out of there. We were happy to get back to my house that afternoon to laugh nervously telling my brother about the caper. He called it bullshit! Yeah two weeks later my brother and his friend were telling me about the two guys chasing them off the fucking catwalk too!! Yeah, was it bullshit then?

A year later orange and white construction barrels were like ornaments on the bridge for repair work being performed. I was in the passenger seat of my buddy Paul's car coming home from New Bedford. It was an orange Nova his grand dad had given him. For some reason who knows to this day why, Paul snapped halfway over the bridge. He decided to start using the car as a battering ram and started crashing the barrels. Barrels made of metal back then just smashing out of the way and flying one by one. The fact though they were all being hit on my side had me with my feet on the dash yelling holy shit!! I couldn't even get a what 'da fuck out of my mouth before he had hit five of the bastards! I will be honest I have no idea how many he hit but when we got back to the bowling alley the radiator was steaming. Paul parked in the very spot he always did, right in front. We got out and he never even looked back at the car. I don't think I stopped looking at it for fifteen minutes in amazement that this fucking nut just cracked all them barrels, holy shit, fun times! Paul was a always a blast!

In '96' heading home one night real late coming from the Cape, I was cruising with the top down in my old '71' Corvette Convertible. I was just coming onto the span of the Braga heading west in the center lane doing seventy miles per hour or so, it happened!! I saw something come on my drivers side really fast just able to look fast enough to see numbers on the front fender. A state cop! In a millisecond a click on the loudspeaker I heard him say, "let's run that fucking RAT!". He kept screwing speeding away from me hit the lights fast and turned them off. Well that fuck, I thought. It's on! I booted that bitch as fast as the fucker would go. I only had a small block and this fucker had some big police package I am sure. He obviously had run my plate already because he drove me escort to my house. When I pulled on the side of the cruiser in the street it turned out to be a nephew of an old girlfriend. I could tell the first second by his patented smile. We had quick catch up conversations that were fun and then he was on his way.

Oh boy '98' brought me to wonder if the bridge and immediate area thereabouts weren't trying to kill me. Heading home again late around one in the morning from the New Bedford the smash happened so fast! It sounded like I just got shot! There was a gaping hole in the middle of the windshield. Listen, you know how hard it is to break a windshield never mind blow a hole in it. This is all going on while driving 75 or 80 mph, thank goodness I was in the middle lane before this. Where am I now?? I was all about trying to be on the brakes as I was looking to see what was stinging my right arm. Looking down toward it though and into the back area of the car being only a two seater, my Reatta didn't have a back seat, it was a flat deck. That's where the boulder came to rest! The top of the bridge vantage point by slowing down looking back in the drivers door rear view mirror revealed the fucking asshole that threw it. On the overpass were two people one having a red and black stripped item of clothing on. I grabbed my cellphone to call 911 while driving looking out the hole in the middle of the windshield. I drove around all the exits to go back over the bridge to get them. I told the cops they better beat me there too, because things are going to get really ugly! Those two fucking little thugs didn't even get to Denny's before I ended up running the front of my car into them two stupid fucks on the sidewalk! As the State cop cruiser pulled up I figured it was going to be a night in the gray bar hotel. To my total disbelief that cop asked me if the car would still drive. Well hell, I was feeling that he was a fan of Clint Eastwood movies too! He said to get it the fuck out of here before any city cops get here. He didn't tell me twice!

March '99' around four fifty nine pm that afternoon I was driving west again from Westport. I had just dropped a buddy Bobby off that was carpooling to his house. On the way back home to Somerset the thing we had always joked about as a kid happened! I had a rental truck as my car was having service work done at a dealership. I was driving in the center lane just starting to come under the city hall when it became mayhem! Ten concrete panels came loose from the ceiling in the tunnel and fell onto the highway below. I know some angel had to be on my shoulders cause the minivan on the side of me got hit by it, and I just escaped him being shoved and rolled into my lane. The traffic behind the carnage was halting and I know that I was the only one driving over the bridge now. I jumped on my phone and called Bobby, "fuck off the city hall over the highway almost just got me buddy!" I told him to flick on the TV there was going to be big news I am sure. Minutes after I got home it was already on the news.

It just took the city fourteen years to fix the fucking thing and open the whole bridge again!

Saturday morning in early summer '09' that bridge tried maybe for it's last time to get me. I was just going for a nice bridges ride that I like to take. It starts way down north in my town with a little swivel bridge that spans the river near a local agricultural school. The next place to head from there, was to come back over the next bridge on the river heading toward Newport which was the Brightman. Crossing that one gets better because from there you can see almost all of them you would ride over in the next five hours of the 'bridges tour'. Jumping on 195 east heading toward Fall River I couldn't help but do the scenery scan about me, while blasting along at about eighty mph. The engine on that bike just has a beautiful low melodic hum at eighty to eighty five, ah I am loving this. Almost as usual the bridge had construction going on. This time it was painting it blue from its signature green it had been from it's inception. The right lane had plastic barrels blocking it off, so only the middle and high speed lanes were available coming from the west. After the center span that was being painted the highway opened up because of the exit still open at the end of the bridge, thank God! I never ride on the side of anyone. I just think if mechanical failure happens, or they decide to drop their fucking phone, I will not die. I had just passed this car in the center lane on the incline, just as we got to the top of the span I hit the blinker to get back in front of him. When I just got back in the center lane the, 'boom' was a familiar sound of the rear tire blowing, like in Florida a few years before! The life in front of your eyes situation again! Wrestling that bitch all the way down to the first exit 'V' on the highway is where I landed. Still on two wheels was the most amazing fucking thing again! Did I just fucking survive another blow out again? As to the same tee, the driver I passed that almost creamed me pulled over to compliment the driving. I just asked him to hold so I could get off of the thing then have a heart attack. A lot of nervous laughter between us before he would head on his way. The rest of the ride never happened that day as it took all day for the local Harley place to pick me up and get a new tire on. Five o'clock came as they were closing I was leaving and heading back home into some black clouds. Fuck I was thinking I already survived my 'black cloud' for the day! Before I left I put all the rain gear on though just in case and my helmet with a brim. Great idea as it seems. Oh you will not guess where the heavens opened up on me. Right at the top of the fucking Braga Bridge! Obviously this fucking thing hates me as I just hydroplaned all the way down the bridge to my home town. I always got asked when I got in how the ride was. 'Unfuckingbelievable!!!' was the only answer! Yeah, fun times!!

HOT FUN
SUMMER FUN TIMES

Come on hurry the hell up! I have to get out of here I have places to be! That's all I could think on this Friday. It was almost quitting time and it's hot. It was mid-summer of 2012 and that night I was going to make my annual pilgrimage to Ocean Park in New London, Connecticut. My best buddy Eddie played in a band that rocks that place every year. Ocean Park is a beach positioned where you can see points of Groton, Connecticut to the left and Long Island to the right far in the distance. Sitting on the benches by the water at night you can follow the lights on the Long Island Ferry for just about it's whole journey. There is a huge boardwalk with an elevated performing stage in the center lit at night for the concert series. At one end of the park are carnival rides and a food pavilion not far from the band stage. An upstairs bar with a nice balcony to view the action would always find me there. I got home from work on that Friday and took an ice cold shower to get the body going again after a long day doing carpentry. Now it was time to get on the road heading to New London.

As I stood in the garage gazing at my two awesome machines the Harley won the coin toss. I was glad it did with the shear heat of the six o'clock hour we were still about ninety-nine degrees. The engine came to life with her usual rumble of the house. I rode out early that evening onto the highway that just radiated the heat. It was making the ride feel much like being in the Florida Keys. Usually I ride with a helmet on all the time but tonight I could not wait to get out to RI to get this thing off! I jumped off the highway closer to Providence than the further south I normally would to get fuel as I was really low. This would turn out to be critical later. I try to stay away from gas stations in the middle of the night coming home, it keeps life simple. Fueling while standing her straight up was the order here to have enough gas to get back home tonight according to the normal plan. I packed the helmet away for a cooler hour or so cruise heading south for a great night of music, friends, and fun.

Navigating New London is like a maze. It has many intersections that have complicated street crossing hubs. I remember the first time going to a job there it was a nightmare. I had done many projects in the city which helped me to know the shortcuts. Some of them though, took you through rather seedy areas of town. I figured 'fuck with no one', and I'd have no problems. The last major crazy intersection heading out toward the park is a three lane crossover at an angle. On a bike you better watch the assholes, seems someone is not looking there all the time. Tonight was no different my friend. I just waved the asshole by and gave them a half peace sign and an idea of their heritage with donkeys. The last road heading down to the beach has a small neighborhood feel to it. Small ranch houses built in the late 50's adorn the streets until the end of the road came to a single traffic light to take the right into the park. Pulling up to the pay booths the kid loved the bike, so I just got the wave in. I ran down the third row all the way to the premier parking spot at the end of the row closest to the band stage. I couldn't believe I was the only bike here. By the time I locked up and got ready for fun I was surrounded like I brought a crowd of two wheeled maniacs parked all around me.

The band was just starting their first tune, an instrumental to let the sound guy get it all right before the singer takes over. During that I made my usual gestures to all in the band as I went by the stage to the soundboard to say hi to friends. I was glad I was there in time for Eddie to sing a great song I liked and that got the night going for me. I spent the rest of the evening talking with friends, eating like a fool, and yes a few beers. The best part about band break that evening besides talking with the guys in the band as they came off stage, were the fireworks. A real serious half hour display in all its glory gets all the onlookers rooting, screaming, and all the car horns tooting for sure. A total highlight every year near the end of the evening the band does a song 'Hot Fun in the Summertime'. The whole scene is quintessential to the facts your actually living the song at 'that' moment. It's almost worthy of a movie scene. It's a warm summer evening almost midnight on the boardwalk by the water watching the ferries making their way to and from Long Island listening to a great band too. What could go wrong? I'm living the good life here!

As the band finished the night with all goodbyes said, I headed back to my magic carpet ride to go home. All the other bikes had left early as mine was there alone. Still being very warm that night close to midnight I opted to leave the helmet in the trunk of the bike. I figured when I get to Mass., I will make the stop to put it back on for legality sake. I got ready and fired that engine with that nice deep roar. My buddies that ride in the band still had live mics on stage, and I heard a 'shiny side up joke'. Thank goodness there were no cars still parked in front of me or anything for that fact. I put up the kick-stand and clicked her down into first gear. As I let out the clutch half way out the cable broke! The bitch launched off instead of chugging out. Holy shit! The clutch handle just slammed the handlebar and was loose without engaging. This is really not fucking good. I can't stop this bitch now, a bike towed from New London to home would be a fortune. No helmet on, fuck! Oh well Mass. helmet law is the least of my worries, I have to get there first! I had to travel the lanes of the lot up and down in first gear until I figured I am not wait-ing for the traffic leaving the 'out' lane only. I took the 'in' lane and had cops fucking screaming bloody murder at me. I just screamed "clutch broke and going to Mass.!".

Slam shifting that bike up into second gear I got to the traffic light at the top of the road with the 'red' my way. Awesome I figured as I just drove up the left of the line of stopped traffic since it was the loneliest intersection in New London. I just banged a left hand turn heading home ahead of the line of traffic who must have thought, 'this biker is an asshole'! The fun begins up the road where now I cannot stop at any cost and have to negotiate five killer intersections on a good day, no less tonight without a clutch! When I got to the major angled intersection, crossing three of my lanes to get over to the three oncoming killer lanes was the eye opener. I just managed to have a guy notice me as I cut him off. The way he jerked to the left stopped the other two lanes which let me pull my maneuver flaw-lessly. The oncoming traffic wasn't quite so easy but vehicles coming my way didn't want to hit a Harley. I got by though but was coming to three lights in a row with a lot of cross traffic. The first red light I managed to run with out incident bringing me into the crack house area of town. Slowing down coming upon the second light I snapped the gears down using rpms only to shift her. I had to make a right hand turn. The traffic would have killed me for sure and I did two more runs around that block until I actually got a green light, yeah! Saying good bye to the crack head part of town was great only to get to the maze of the five way intersection. I had to go diagonally across this one again but did so against the red light before the other traffic moved, the aggressor wins tonight! Now I only had a few more major moves and I might get to the highway. I came down the hill toward the police station entrance where another three lanes of one way high speed traffic is coming. I have to take a sharp left. There is no escape and I am heading against the light, it's red oh no! Jamming this bitch down to first and just about lugging along, the light turned almost as it was too late. Making that left was huge, now I just had to try to make it home as I made the right up onto the highway.

I got up to speed just making the legal limit, I had to save gas. Doing a little calculation it proved just those few early exits coming down for the evening putting in gas too soon was going to fuck me going home. I could not stop, there would be no getting a full dresser with this weight on the road again if I did. It would just chunk to a stop, and maybe cause me to drop her which was non fucking acceptable! I listened to the satellite radio riding really slow around fifty five as to not eat gas mileage. It was awesome for a great warm night and I didn't put too much more into it until I took the right turn at Providence heading over to the Mass. line towards home. I never felt so paranoid as I did riding that night without a helmet after crossing into Mass. If I just have enough gas, fuck! When I got to the route 136 exit the bike bogged down, it was the gas. Flipping the gas switch over to get most of that last gas was really going to help here. Holy shit I don't think I can make it. I let off the gas even more to about forty five on the highway no less, glad it was really late with no traffic. There's the home exit. I could not help but get a bit excited thinking I may make it with no clutch! Nobody was coming in either direction off the exit to let me make the right out toward route 103, I was getting closer. A real 'classic fucked move', gave me the left onto route 103 in front of some asshole screaming yelling and tooting the horn. I'm just glad he wasn't drunk and gave me the 'chrome horn'! I drove right in front of the guy! One more turn onto my street, if I can just get over this hill to get there.

The police always sit at the top of that hill late evenings running license plates coming into town and checking out all that show up at the traffic light. As I came chugging up the hill the light was red. I had slammed that gear down ahead of time so I could do the fake 'this helmet is driving me crazy arm up by the side of the head', to block his sight. I think the fucker was sleeping cause he didn't even look at me. Just down the hill to the sweeping left by the nursing home to my street. Three cars coming my way made me have to ride down to the rotary to come back around and take a right onto my street. Slowly I made it up my street still hoping for the gas to make it. I got a flutter of the engine two houses short of mine still down the hill. I jammed the gas and shifted up to third gear. As I took the left into my driveway, it ran out of gas. I was trying but not able to get her into neutral to have an easy stop of it. Life would not let that happen. Instead the bike came to a chugging suffocating halt fairly abruptly in the driveway, five feet from the garage door. Fucking 'eh!! I made it, you stubborn mother I was thinking. Five or six times on that ride home I got real lucky. That was some 'Hot Fun' that summertime night for me. As I went off to sleep that night the sound of the band playing that song in my head summed up the evening, 'Hot Fun in the Summertime!', I love my life!!

BLOOD BROTHERS
SENT BY ANGELS

Holy Shit, we're in the racing news? Kenny came up with the photo evidence! We stood in my office laughing until tears were in our frigging eyes. He could come up with some shit! It started two years earlier when a fellow came in looking for a sales job at the dealership. He explained how he had been around the business for a number of years. He also told me how much of a race fan he was. He bragged about his brothers that raced the local kids on the avenue in Fall River. I was thinking I should know this guy but no bells rang in my head. A short interview later revealed the shoulder length hair this guy had. Silver gray straight as an arrow. Shoulder fucking length in a Buick dealership!? Holy Shit I will have a hard time selling the 'old man' on this guy. I really have no idea why but the next morning I went to bat up in the office for the new guy I thought could light things up. Twenty minutes of a story and I had the go ahead to bring him on but I really didn't share the whole story with the old man. I called Kenny that afternoon and told him he was on. One caveat though was he buy a hat and hide that hair until he sold sixteen cars. On that day we'd surprise the old man and let it come down baby! The fix was in, he was to start in the morning.

The very next morning Kenny showed up early. We got everything he would need to be a sales movie star. Hey buddy good job with the hair under the hat! If I hadn't seen the hair to his shoulders two days ago I wouldn't have believed it looking at him now. Within an hour he landed a customer out of service and was selling a GTA that really needed to leave the lot. That afternoon two of his appointments showed, and that was three for the first day. I met him later for a drink and his goal was, hat off in three weeks. I will say this, he did it in fucking one! This guy walked into a pretty sleepy easygoing place like ours, and just did sixteen in a week! That night at the bar we agreed to let that hair fly tomorrow. Uh oh here we go in the morning, I can already hear the page to the old man's office.

The next day I came in, Kenny already had a service customer pretty much wrapped up to purchase a truck. Timing could not have been better than for him to come to the sales desk at the same time the old man was walking in the door for the day. Good mornings aside I will tell you this, it was a shock to see the old man's face when Kenny took that hat off. Ken says, "hey Gerard", not my name by the way, but that's what he called me all the time. "I have one in the bank extra for the hat toss!" He threw the hat in the chair. His shoulder length hair came down just as straight, silver, and I must say, long! Oh boy I could see the old man's eyes open up to the size of a cue ball. "Gerry can I see you in my office", the old man said. So that went well I'm thinking. Upon arrival in the old man's office that's all I could do was say, "I know, I know." Ten minutes of describing how he sells like a fucking machine got me and Ken out of that one. Then, oh yeah, we were on to some fun times!

A Sunday found just me and Kenny working as they were very slow days. It was the beginning for the car dealerships to start opening on Sundays. Ken saw me going to the trunk of my black Reatta only to come out with a set of golf clubs. What the hell are you doing with them my friend 'playing through'? No buddy, what I am doing is bringing these over in the showroom. Watch this! I then opened the double doors in the front of the showroom facing the Standard Times building across the field. There was an old abandon farm lot between the dealership lot and the street with a barn silo. I said to him if today was going to ruin my golfing time I'd just get a few hits in here. In the showroom? Well not exactly. I'm going to hit from in the showroom right here. Yep, it's going to slide right by the flag pole eight feet from the doors. Then my friend with any luck right over the new car inventory. If I have any more luck I can sink it into that hole in the top of the barn silo! What do ya think? I knew Kenny was wild but he wasn't looking too happy right that moment as I took my first swing. 'Pop', it went flying out of the showroom. It seemed so much faster than outside on the golf course to me. Right by the flag pole by fucking inches. I could just imagine it hitting the pole and coming back to smash one of the front six by ten glass window panes. That would be a pip to explain to the old man for sure. When the ball passed the pole it was on its way over the brand new Buick inventory. Holy shit, nice hit but it landed a few yards short. When I went for the next one the laughter was so intense I sculled the ball right off the hood of a Park Avenue. The ball still made it out into the field but no where near the silo. The tenth hit had me finally ace the hole in the top of the silo. Kenny then decided to jump in the act. I asked if he played golf at all. He told me never once in his life, but he was playing now! I got one ball ready on the portable tee I had improvised. Kenny took the swing of his life. Yeah baby it went like a frigging rocket! It flew! It flew into that flag pole I was talking about right in front of the show room doors. It smacked that pole so fast and came straight back in the showroom! It came back right over Kenny's head and if it had hit him, it would have fucking killed him for sure. Instead it hit the wall right over an office window in the back of the showroom. It left a hell of a digger in the sheet rock but had enough inertia to fly right back out the front door bouncing on the floor by us! I do believe we both pissed ourselves laughing at the whole scene. There I was putting the Park Avenue in the body shop for a hood fix. That Monday night after the old man left I put a ladder up, and fixed the hole. As I was fixing the hole we had the sales staff laughing their fool asses off telling them the story. We did other crazy stunts too.

One other Sunday before we even decided what to eat for lunch Ken asked a question of me. "Did you have a brother CW?" I couldn't figure where the fuck that question came from! "Yes I did, and he passed away buddy", I told him. "How would you know that", I asked him. He revealed that he and my brother were friends as kids. When our family lived in Tiverton, he and my brother sliced their hands with a knife and did the whole thing like you'd see in an old western movie. Ken proceeded to tell me about the things he and my late bro did when they were kids. It was a hoot to say the least, but one quick call could verify this I bet. I dialed the phone on the sales desk and hit speaker. My sister answered the phone with her normal salutations and I got right into it. "Hey Pat would you know anybody by the name of Kenny that was CW's friend growing up in Tiverton?". I didn't even get the whole question out when she said, "that fat fuck sat on my favorite lunchbox when we were kids!" He crushed her lunchbox screwing around with my brother that morning. I hung up the phone, and it seems like at that second he and I became real close. Ken said he had put that together in his head the day he came looking for the job when he saw my last name, but never wanted to ask. He had heard through a friend, and came to the wake. So many people were there, and I was in a fog, I could not remember. That night at home I looked, I saw his name in the visitors book from the wake. Maybe CW brought this sick bastard to me to have some fun, who knows right?!

Speaking of fun it never stopped around Kenny. One Saturday late in the afternoon it was just he and I as every one had been pardoned for the day. A young kid pulled up with his car he had been building for racing. Ken said worry nothing this kid is outta here. The showroom had a White Formula 350 with tee tops sitting right by the side door. It was like a homing device for those kids. They jumped out of their car in the lot and basically just about ran into the showroom to look at this Formula. Conversations of the engine the kid had just put dropped in the car in front of the showroom. It all boiled down to we had twenty minutes left to be here and this kid wants to race! The eye contact between two wild men had me opening the showroom doors as Kenny fired up the Formula. I had just cleared the second door opening when I heard the screech. Ken peeled out of the showroom from where it was fucking parked!! What 'da fuck you should have seen the tire smoke in the building rising up into the offices, holy shit am I fucked! The plan was for Ken and the kid to show up at the lights on route 240 and take the green. I would be standing in the bed of a pickup at the dealership sign out toward the highway to call the winner. I could hear them both while they had the red light, burning up the tires for traction when the light turned. It's Green! Here we come, and I can not believe we beat the frigging kid by a hood length for fifty bucks! It was more about the win, than the fifty you can believe me! Thank goodness I had sold plenty of vehicles to the fire dept. and firemen in the town. I had several of them there until almost nine that night with big fans blowing the smoke out of the building and offices upstairs. The next morning found me there gluing back the carpet Ken scooted out behind the car when he took off out of the showroom. Oh no, I will never be able to hide the peel out marks in a huge half circle out of the showroom into the lot! Ken was really excited to go kick those kids ass and I hadn't even thought of warning him not to do that shit. It was only minutes when the old man was paging me to his office. He didn't mention the smoke. He didn't mention the peel marks either. He did though drop a piece of the rubber he took off the rear wheel wells onto his desk then leaned back in his seat to ask. "Do you mind at least telling me what the hell went on here?" I kind of denied it ever happened for about ten seconds. As I saw redness building on his forehead I grabbed the fifty and threw it on his desk. "Yeah we won, and yeah you greedy fuck you can keep it!" I still tell the story to the newbies in the business when we are talking about things you 'used' to do.

Ken came in the office to tell me he got the old man to let us off together on a Saturday. Really, in the car biz you got us both off? That Saturday found us on the way to the northern nationals for drag racing in New Hampshire. We took Ken's brand new Formula he had just bought for the ride. Ken pulled over at some dunkin' donuts half way to the track to 'freshen up' the car. He rubbed the fucking car so much I smoked two joints watching. The cops in the drive up smelled it for sure and gave me the 'no' head nod to make the second one come to an early end with a major heart rush! At the track we bought pit passes to enjoy the excitement closer to the action, and smell some race fumes. Paul Romine won the championship that day. Timing is everything. Ken and I were there as the race vehicle arrived at the pits. Paul stood up with Kenny pulling him out of the seat. The man from the racing league handed Paul the trophy and then Paul turned to shake my hand! So the picture on the front of the paper was Paul with the trophy shaking my hand and Ken standing with his hand on Paul's shoulder. If Romine ever saw the picture he must have thought, who the fuck are those two guys? The laughter out of me and Ken looking at that damn picture! That picture in my office kept the laughter alive. Ken passed away suddenly, a total shock! The pipeline made it possible for me though because I got to know the 'Blood Brother'! I'm frigging glad I did!

MAKIN' IT BACK
KISS THE GROUND

Get out! Holy shit there we were standing on the sidewalk in Boston. He drove away! I was thinking he would be coming back around the block or something. My brother would always pull something on you to see what you were made of. This time is was me and my buddy Al. It was another Saturday afternoon cruise to the Boston music stores. We would go to basically play every instrument on the floor like a band to have some fun. Buying something wasn't even on the list, it was just a frigging blast. Where else can you try the latest instruments possible that are brand new. It was amazing how many great players were in these stores on a weekend afternoon. We had a great time the three of us just beating things up and then a quick lunch. During lunch Al and I just kept messing with my brother CW to the point he just gave one of the very slight throat clearing sounds. Yeah, that's how you know you have him! The tormenting of CW just was incredible until just about a block away from Chinatown the car came to a slamming, skidding fucking halt! That's when he ejected us! Yep, get out were his last words as he pulled away! Al and I started laughing like a bastard. We thought he'd come back as soon as he left, but then saw the right hand turn onto the highway heading home. Holy shit, he took the highway!

Al's hand went up and flagged a taxi as fast as you could say, 'what the fuck?' As the taxi pulled over and the window came down Al screamed, "huge tip to go to Somerset NOW!" "Get the fuck in", the guy said and we were now on the highway too! Al basically said we had to beat an asshole that just dropped us off as a joke, and it was going to be well worth the tip. The driver liked the sound of that, and it wasn't long before we passed my silly ass stupid fuck brother driving in the low speed lane at fifty five miles per hour. We were doing eighty and this was going to be good! When we got to Somerset we had the driver drop us off at my house. It was going to be great to see the look on a guy that fucked us as we beat him home fifty two miles from Boston. The best part is my mother had just finished baking a cake. We both had a huge piece of hot nice fresh cake on the plate as CW came sauntering in. He looked like he saw a ghost! Nice! We never told that asshole how we were to make it back before him either. He asked me about thirty times too, he never got that answer.

On a fantastic summer day a friend Joey and I were to head out for a scuba dive off my boat. He was a great open water diver so the goal for this dive would be a big journey. I had planned a trip to the sunken U-853, a German submarine off the coast of Block Island. It sits in one hundred and twenty one feet of water. It had been sunk the day before Germany surrendered. It sits on the bottom almost perfectly straight up seven miles off of Block Island. It's a very technical dive also because of bottom times, depths and pressures involved. When we arrived we had a plan to run over in case of any possible thing going wrong. We pitched the plan back and forth to each other while gearing up for the incredible journey into the dark abyss. Below the depth of sixty or so feet, the natural light from the surface and our sun disappears and now you're on your own. Our dive lights fired up as we just dropped like a free fall sky diving, but this one is in ultra slow motion! There she is! At about eighty five or ninety feet the shadow of German harassment and death comes into view. As ugly, is as beautiful as she may be, sitting there silently rotting away into the chasm of time. I remember Joey's wide open eyes as he looked at me that afternoon witnessing history. He had his tablet out writing, fucking awesome! Yes, yes it was! It was time to go already, according to the plan. Without fail we slowly headed up and watched a piece of the past turn into darkness behind us. There were two stops on the way up to tie off for decompression times. Joey wrote notes during that time about becoming an onboard flight engineer for the airlines. Really? He already had the plan he was executing soon. Upon arrival at the surface, I laughed telling him I had never had such a conversation decompressing before. It was time to get back before big winds came and setting sun.

It wasn't long into dragging in the massive amount of anchor line before I noticed we were overheating the engine, and a knock was getting louder. Drifting out in open water is not going to be an option here. 'Alright Mr. onboard flight engineer what's your take.' I was throwing it all on Joey with a laugh, oh fuck yeah, a nervous laugh! We got that engine cover up and that guy went to work. With a minor tool set he was able to diagnose the flywheel being the problem. It seemed like no time at all we were ready to fire the engine to see the temps drop immediately right back to normal, and no knock either. Yeah we joked like hell talking about being a dumb bastard with no tools out here twenty miles off shore drifting with no hope. Joey went onto the new career of an onboard flight engineer. One of our next awesome conversations many years later of him saving a jet one night over the ocean made me proud. His eyes were wide as I told him about a few of the times on aircraft since I saw him last.

I got the call. It was from my commander from the tactical communications unit. I had three hours to get all the communications gear and our crew on planes heading 'somewhere' in the world. As part of the Rapid Deployment Force it is not an option to be late. I saw the massive C-5 coming to a halt, with the giant nose rising into the air exposing the loading deck. The massive plane even lowered it's suspension to take on the load we had coming in. The load master, who is in total control, went over the plan to put our two tractor trailers, four deuce and a half trucks and three jeeps in this plane. So impressive to see military might in play as we closed the nose and got ready for take off. A few minutes into the flight had the crew bringing us up to the galley for a great meal you would never think was coming. Then we got our orders. It kind of made your stomach 'not right' but you always act like it's not a problem. After chow we all dispersed into different areas of the plane. I always loved to go in the cockpit to watch the activity. This day was no different as we were about to in flight refuel. A load like ours was to heavy to take off with a full load of fuel also. The plane couldn't get off the runway fast enough. I have to say if you have seen it a million times, it's awesome in the captain's chair, as that frigging fueling boom goes over your head and slam-bangs into the receiving pocket for it's thousands of pounds of fuel. Now the dry mass of this plane is like one hundred sixty five tons, plus our equipment, and another eighty thousand pounds of fuel additional we just took on. I watched as the KC-135 pulled away from us to the left for his next refueling rendezvous. We were on our way now gaining some altitude and speed to meet our expected co:ordinances by the next day.

I couldn't help but look at the onboard engineer thinking this is what my buddy Joey is doing for a living now. I don't think it could have been twenty minutes when I heard something 'not normal' on a plane to me anyway. Yeah I heard, 'lost engine two, fire out, I shut her down!' coming from Mr. fucking onboard engineer! I'm wanting to scream, what? You just lost a fucking engine over the northern Atlantic Ocean and your just fucking hunky dory with shutting the fucking thing down?! No one in the cockpit was even phased! This pilot, co pilot, commander and engineer acted like they had just received a dry cleaning ticket fucking stub! NO reaction from either of them. My heart was pounding. I guess they realized they were freezing me out when the co-pilot said to me they can fly on two engines but landing is a major problem! The rest of them all laughed when he said that. There was something about the laugh that said they've done that shit before. Yeah I gauged it as the nervous laugh too!

No, are you shitting me?!! What the fuck?!! I was starting to think I picked the absolute wrong place to hang on this frigging mission. What the hell? Uh oh, it looks like we are about to do the 'tough landing' deal. We just lost another engine! It was midnight and just coming over Europe we were not going to be able to land at the destination planned, we might not even make it there. Fast talking on the pilot's part had us limping into Germany at a major military installation with emergency gear at the ready. When we landed we slid the runway all the way to the past outrun grass without going into the ditch. Whew, what a heavy fucking plane I heard, as the two engines remaining in reverse were roaring to stop us! Again after the halt the whole crew looked like it was a nothing~burger! Who the hell are these people I thought! We exited the plane only to have one of our guys almost get us shot because he went over behind the wheel of the aircraft to take a piss. We could only hear M-16's shucking up as the security police were yelling freeze!! They should have shot that asshole Murray, he almost killed us at the firing range one day. What the fuck! It took an hour to get enough paperwork and ID's produced to finally get our hands down. This was the eighties before all the major terrorist shit. It was just a plane that showed up unannounced now with people around the runway. Good job done, the police put us up at the Amelia Earhart hotel where the American Iran Hostages had been the week before. It wasn't fifteen minutes when the Security Police with bomb sniffing dogs showed up in the lobby. I was having another major rush, and I didn't even have any pot! They were here to investigate the mysterious unidentified package called in by someone! Murray noticed a strange bag with ours and called them! Holy shit! Only to find the ID on the bag saying Dover AFB, where the C-5 came from that brought us. It was a crew shaving bag. Oh yeah, I was on the phone to my commander stateside to take Murray out of the program because we were about to shoot him, before he had us killed!

Repairs in hand had us on the way in six hours. Murray stayed in Germany, so we didn't get killed because of him while performing our mission. Months later, with sand in everything you owned, we left on a C-130 to head home. This baby had no comfort level at all. Very cold, and very loud! It was going to be a long thirty six or more hour flight. Fuck it, I'm going home! I didn't give a shit if it was a Yugo, I wanted to go home! It would take probably three in-flight refueling procedures to get us home on this long flight. I had everything like sleeping bags to keep warm, you become creative to get home and don't bitch! It really started to suck when the plane started, 'not sounding right' compared to the vibration that was ringing in your head. Not again, are you shitting me? Yeah we were out over the Atlantic and couldn't make Greenland. Fast Air Force maneuvers had us just able to limp back and make it over the volcanic peaks of the islands in Portugal for an emergency landing. I was really starting to fucking hate planes! We stayed on the runway sleeping in the heat for three days awaiting parts and techs to fix the plane to be flown in. I will say, I did get to sneak to a bull fight. The place also had the best rainbows every morning because of the volcanic mountains deflecting the moisture from the ocean air into the sunrise. To never be forgotten, I was just in awe of it's beauty. We were glad the rest of the trip was boring for a change. Always though, when that plane landed and the mission was over, the first thing I did was drop to my knees and kiss the American soil. I was just happy I was ~makin' it back~ to all I knew and loved!!

UNTIL THEY COME
WILD TIMES IN BANDS

Don't move! The cows were running by both sides of us. "Holy shit", my brother yelled "I didn't think that she could do that so quick!" Tina our dog was herding the cows in the field behind our house. Problem is, we were in the way! These animals to our surprise, were so used to humans they would never stampede us. The after school fun would be to venture out to the fields and find out what was happening in the near wilderness. Wilderness, yeah right, about six huge grass fields connected to five wooded areas. The whole area combined could have been six square miles, oh yeah, six for fun! We spent many a day out there growing up. We flew hand made kites with eight reels of line, with tails as long as the amount of material you could steal! The beat up wet kite would always manage to last until they would be calling you home for supper. We had many a camp fire out there too. One day the wind was blowing like crazy, but being kids who would think a little fire grows fast. Really frigging fast!

The next thing I knew, that fire blew up and singed my eye brows. Holy shit it was flaming up in the trees over our head too!

Run! We ran our fucking fool asses out of the field heading to the house. When we got there I screamed at my sister to call the fire department because we saw a fire in the field behind the house! I remember trying to figure out how to get the burn smell out of my eyebrows as they were like an eighth of an inch long with burn ball wads at the ends and smelling like burned skin. A great shower before supper and dowsing the clothes in the laundry made me feel like I got away with that one, until the cops showed at the door asking questions. Yeah, until they came I was the cat's ass. Five minutes later I was the biggest asshole in the neighborhood in my parents eyes, but the cops never knew. They didn't turn me in. The old man told me later it was obvious when I had no eyebrows or eyelashes left, I was the culprit! He took a big puff off his L&M and laughed!

A few years later I had the great fortune to play in my brother's band. The first number of gigs were either private parties or a fantastic rustic club on Martha's Vineyard. We always basically knew the crowd and it was easy for a young schmuck like me to get used to playing the drums, and trying to sing also. CW always reminded me, 'not to let the words get in the way of a good song'. The prick! How the hell could I be good, I was a kid! He didn't want to hear it, get it fucking right! The place we considered one of our old home clubs though was 'The Howard Lounge'. The place was an absolute dive. It was in Buzzards Bay on the inclined on ramp to the Bourne Bridge. It was owned by a four foot four inch full blooded Indian lady that didn't give a shit for nothin'! When you would ask Julie for a drink, good luck if you were in the band! I just brought my own, I figured that out early. The place had a great pool table down the back of the club. I found it funny to sink the eight ball on the break playing the adults in the club, when they could not. Thanks dad for that real quick education at six on our table at home, it has payed off plenty in life!

The fun about the Howard was the crowd. There was an interesting mix of cooped up cape coders, and transient tourists trying to get laid. The interesting part of the mix though was the service guys from the base up the road a few miles. One fun Friday night we were about to start for the evening. We didn't have a programmed show, but pretty much always started with an old fifty's tune, Rock Around the Clock. When we got the the first phrase of the song the dance floor was full. I was thinking, wow this is gonna be a fun night. The second phrase of the song rang out with it's quick stanza. Wouldn't ya know by the third line, the whole dance floor broke out in a fight! It was like 'all fall down!'. Guys were whacking chicks, and girls were kicking and beating guys! I couldn't fucking believe my brother kept singing. I looked at him and them with total panic. When he had a second he leaned back and said, "they love us, and don't do anything 'until they come' for us!". He had the silliest fucking stupid laugh when he said it too. I realized, yup, I entertain fucking drunks for a living! I guess I realized at that point, soooo early in life, I was on the way to fun times!

The band played many gigs for years and we always managed to laugh at the night we called the 'all fall down' fight. I could not believe there were locks of hair on the floor, and ten were yanked out of there to the clink that night! Where else could you get that entertainment for fifty bucks a guy! The Howard was always our fun place to call home. Fun times also led us to a few weddings we were hired to provide the entertainment. We usually would set up a few hours before anyone would ever get to the hall of the reception. The last thing you want is a band setting up as the bridal party is entering the building. Today though was a bit different. People were already showing up to the reception hall at the time the wedding was supposedly happening. I remember the guitar player Nino saying to me, "hey Ger, they'll be separated before they cut the cake!". What a fucking laugh we all broke into. We didn't even fucking care either, because my bro was excellent at always grabbing all the cash before an event ever happened!

The crowd started to file in and we decided to give it a little easy background music. People didn't mingle or talk like usual. They just seemed to go to the bar a few times and go directly to the opposing sides. Yeah, at this wedding there was a 'He' and 'She' side of the room. About the third instrumental we had played, Nino was already starting. He was talking to me on the side how they'd be separated before cutting the cake! CW was on the other side telling me this looked like 'all fall down' night. I can't believe both them assholes called it! Within about four bars into the next song a wad of mashed potatoes went flying across the room! Nino looked back at me! When we met eyes I could not even fucking believe it was on! A retaliatory strike came with I think it was a bowl of green beans. Oh fuck! This is getting interesting! My brother looked back and started right into, of all things, Rock Around the Clock! I looked at him in amazement and off mic he said, "fuck it, there ain't no fights without our theme song!" We played two more songs before there was no food left to throw, and people were so tired from fighting they were ready to pass the fuck out! Payed already, the groom just told us to hit the road. Yup, CW always said, just keep playing, 'Until They Come' for us!!

BERNIE

TOXIC RELATIONS

Take the gun away from my throat, give me fifteen seconds, and you'll never see us again! Before that statement by nine months and a few weeks, is when this mess all started. I was sitting with a friend one afternoon in an American Legion, enjoying beers and listening to tapes. His tape machine always had some fun stuff of ours on it from the middle of the night recording sessions. We were just laughing at some of the antics that we had got involved with playing in the same band over the years. At that point he suggested that I come to the new year's gig they were playing that evening. There was not too much arm wrenching involved. Within two hours I was home getting some clothes together for this event. I almost did not go when time came. If I hadn't, oh hell, I would have missed all of this?

I got to the party fashionably late and slithered right to the bar. I felt like a great white shark off the beaches of cape cod in 'Jaws' sizing up the crowd for stray single fish. A few sips of beer found my buddy waiving me over to show me where he had, 'set me up'. Yeah, I guess this was perfect I was the only guy at a table of seven women. Nice! Now that is a friend for ya. Yeah think about it later, he must have fucking hated me! The band was great that night and the ladies at the table treated me pretty damn good as they got my food, drinks and all I had to do was dance. Fun evening toward the end had telephone numbers being exchanged with the promise of going out sometime. The very next week had chips being cashed with one of the calls for a date to go see a band. One of my friends and coworkers mixed sound for this local cover band, that was the destination.

We got to the club that evening to find a packed house. Nothing better for a band making the effort than a great crowd. After getting drinks the first thing I had to do was get us positioned near the sound board to sneak up on my buddy working it that night. As the band started it obviously was going to be a wild evening. They were a 'Doors' tribute band, and I must say the first five minutes had me totally blown away. It was like the real frigging thing to me, wow! Three quarters through the first song we were able to finally jostle our way over to the sound board. I used a great body bump to let Wade know that 'some fucking asshole' showed up that never does! It was a fun time, and after all introductions, the band went on to a spectacular first set. At break a conversation between the three of us had me and my buddy already having the perfect name for this one. Oh yeah, with slight refinements I am positive Wade coined it to be 'Boozin', just perfect we would only know later. Oh let the games begin!

A fine Friday afternoon had me heading off the islands. Tonight, was a plan to see The Nakeds, a band my buddy played guitar in. They were a Rhode Island staple as they had been on the scene at that time for about close to forty years. They even went on to be inducted into the R.I. music hall of fame, yeah these guys are the best! A ten piece band that did originals also played Chicago or Tower of Power to perfection. The lead singer, with his patented 'hey neighbor, have a Gansett', raised hell with the crowds every night. It was always exciting to get up to dance when they would start some of their own music from their last CD. This one night would not be any different until they were playing something like, 'Don't Walk Away'. Yeah, this was one of the bands best. The song was written by Clarence Clemons from the 'E' Street band that backed Springsteen. He was a great gentle giant of a man, with a sweet demeanor and fantastic attitude. He joined up with the Nakeds on some of their work, and they gigged together at times, fun fantastic times! After Clarence passed, it was even more special when they would do his songs, so tonight the crowd seemed electric. It was a club in Pawtucket called Corrine's with an awesome packed dance floor. There we were right in front of my buddy Eddie on guitar having a ball dancing. Halfway into the song 'boozin' got her second nick name coined by one of the guys in the band. Yep! The new one got named by the bone player. Right in the middle of the song 'boozin' came up with the slide of the trombone on her arm while on the dance floor. The bone player grabbed it so he could play the solo he had coming up in two bars. He had all he could do to play the frigging solo, he was laughing so hard. He asked me where I found 'spaghetti arms'?!!!

It seemed like a lot of weekends were finding us chasing the band around. A fun place was right down the road from the band leaders house. This early evening had the band opening up the pool party bar area at this local venue. The scene was beautiful as it was a warm sunset and the lights from the band stage gave a neat aura. A great crowd and fun times had the lead singer Steve stripping down at the end of the gig and jumping in the pool for a lap. What the hell, it was open now! I rarely brought my old car to the gigs as I didn't want it left unattended anywhere. Being Rhode Island and knowing what would happen to the thief, the hell with it, I brought it! Above is the perfect picture! In the middle of packing up I talked Steve into making all the guys come out for the picture. Turns out I look at it, and reminisce. One guy left, and came back. One passed, very sad. Three retired. Five crazies are still rocking it today baby! This night is etched in time right here!

The next time they gigged at Effins the band threw a party at the leaders house not far away. The evening again was picture perfection, and again I had the old car too. I got the invite from Steve at break. He looked at me and told me he had to wear a costume to buy beer I liked that afternoon. I wouldn't dare say no to him out of respect, and, oh yeah I like a good time too! When the band broke down we all went to the house where the food and drinks flowed. A big fire got lit out in the back yard pit. The fun time is toward very wee hours of the morning totally drunk watching big speakers from the band burning in the pit. Oh yeah, we're talking this was fucking fun here! Well during one of the rather quiet moments toward dawn, the bass player asked if someone had a cigarette he could bum. Oh yeah it wasn't seconds when a little south Boston accented runty voice of 'booze' came out and said, "it'll stunt your growth!". EWWWW was the crowd reaction, as the guy was kinda short, so..... I just looked at 'boozin' and was wondering why the fuck she couldn't keep that yap shut! Unbelievable! Eddie and I have laughed many times at that night since.

One day while riding the Harley, a great place to stop to eat and drinks had a bunch of Hell's Angels today. I didn't even have a chance to tell the 'booze' to shut up in this place, for things get toxic really quick. While looking at the menu I heard some chick scream at 'booze' who the hell you looking at. I could not even reach to cover her mouth fast enough when I hear from near me, 'YOU!'. It was my frigging trouble maker starting some shit again! The broad started coming around the bar from the other side at a good clip. I was already eyeing my bike to make sure no one had blocked me in. I knew I was going to be leaving this place in how you could say 'a rush'! As that chick went to crack the 'booze' I just misdirected the blow and made her hit the bar. Damn that fucking chick hit harder than guys I had been hit by in bar fights! Let's fucking go, as I grabbed the dummy I was with by the scruff of the coat to run to the bike. That's the fastest

I ever saw that jerk get on the bike, as she fucking knew I was leaving when the engine wound up. Two shot glasses went flying by my face as I was pulling out of the lot with out even looking for traffic oncoming. Great arm, bad aim, again....... unfuckingbelieveable!

The first few weeks of September I would be taking a trip to the car races in Delaware. I usually make it a fun time meeting up with friends, and this time combining it with a great fall bike adventure. I got bitched at until I decided to let her come with me. I knew it was a problem seeing her pack. We're on a bike! So I threw this, that, and the other shit out of the pile and decided what she could take. I should have left her home! Turns out it was freezing that night. This was an eight hour journey on it's best day. Tonight would involve more stops for sure. I was leaving at eleven thirty pm sharp as I needed to be through New York City by a certain time for the toll booths and traffic. I had a lot of fun buzzing down though the tunnels of the Cross Bronx letting that rip and roar of my engine scare the hell out of people in the vehicles next to me. Loud pipes save lives! Coming close to the end of the Jersey pike into Delaware brings on breakfast hunger. I took the first exit to head on my new route finding a place. The truck driver following us for miles couldn't believe 'boozin' was sound asleep on the bike flying down the highway. He asked if I knew it. "Sure" I told him, "but the seat was designed that she would not fall out, I think!" As we laughed! He said "she reminds me of the movie Weekend at Bernie's." Man I have to tell you the two of us broke out into frigging tears laughing. Hence another nick name coined at that instant, 'Bernie'! That one stuck for sure.

The squeaky runty Bostonian accented voice was on the phone again, oh no! A few minutes later her car pulled in the driveway and this time I was going for the ride. We were going to Providence to see the Water Fires event. I had never been and always heard about it, so this would be interesting. As it turns out it was definitely a night for lovers as they were everywhere. A night with a slight chill, but a beautiful clear early evening with slight hues of sunset reflecting off the down town buildings. There were calderas in the river splitting the city that had nice fires lit in them every few hundred feet or so. You could even feel the heat of some of the flames from the shore. There were restaurants set up for the open air atmosphere with huge crowds. It was a very nice and easy going it seemed. It was time to find a drink and some entertainment. We entered a great open court-yard with a local orchestra playing. I was able to grab us a drink from a restaurant nearby and we nestled into a spot with our backs against a chain link fence. There was a construction sight back there blocked off, but it gave us the perfect spot in the back of the venue I thought. A few songs into the performance and our second drink hitting the spot, it happened. Two really nicely dressed couples stood right in front of us. I could not help but thinking, these two guys are real spar cons here. It didn't take long as usual!

'Boozin' kind of poked one of the guys in the back and at the same time told him to slide over he was blocking her, and she was here first. I really was as fucking shocked as he was! The only thing I didn't realize is that within four seconds things changed up 'big time'! He pulled out a fucking gun and put it to my throat, then pushed me to the fence. All the while it seems like maybe a pattern around this fucking chick or something. His buddy became the biggest pick block for any one witnessing this shit. He didn't have a chance to tell me how he was going to throw me in a dumpster or anything before I grabbed 'boozin' by the right fucking ear, and started running. That's right, I told him give me fifteen seconds and he'd never see us again! I was hearing her bitch about the ear grab when some other hero decided he wanted to get involved. He asked me how I'd like to be dragged by the ear. I said to try it but first ask the guy over there with the gun!! I gave an exaggerated point to the direction I had just come running from. It was perfection because he and everyone at that second looked that way. It gave me time for the three stooges escape! Two blocks from the car I dumped her pocketbook to get the keys to her car. Oh yeah if she wasn't in it this time, again she'd be hoofing it! All the way back to my house I explained it to her. I told her Wade named her right, it was 'Boozin'! But then again she earned, 'Spaghetti arms' by herself. I asked her never to come near me again because of the Hell's Angels incident and of course what had just fucking happened! Yeah, I ended all weekends with, 'Bernie'!!

THE BARGE
SURVIVAL DRIFT

Full speed ahead he almost ran us over! What the hell we were yelling! Shining a light at the nut job behind the controls of a Formula thirty-five-foot ocean racing boat almost running over us had no effect! He didn't see us! I can't believe what a cramp in a leg can do while scuba diving, until that day. It happened at least seven hours ago. We had been drifting since a buddy had a leg cramp. I decided not to leave a partner in distress while scuba diving. It felt like days, but I know it was hours. The problem was that now, it was getting dark. Earlier that day we had met on a great afternoon at my boat in Tiverton, Rhode Island. The plan was a fantastic open water dive at a barge a mile and a quarter off the coast of Westport, Mass. It was a fun time securing all the scuba tanks and getting all the gear in the right place for the voyage out to the barge. I know I cracked a joke about the worst thing in the world that could happen, would 'be a fart in a scuba tank', as I tied the last one off. After getting the stupid tears from our eyes from laughing, it was time. The weather was good, and the forecast was to stay that way too. It was time to get fuel, check the ship to shore radio and get this baby going.

The boat was a twenty-four-foot mahogany lap streak Chris Craft built in nineteen sixty one. Yeah she was an old heavy girl. I had changed up the original configuration of the boat to now have a much larger engine with more torque. The weight of all the dive equipment and people too creates a situation in following seas. You always want acceleration and mobility on your side. She was also a single inboard engine so backing in and maneuvering around a fuel dock was always, 'old school'. I loved it. She was painted in a sky blue that beautifully shined. I got tips from an old salt of the sea when going to put the final touches on her. He told me to heat the paint. He gave me some of the same suggestions I always saw my dad use when he painted our house. Maybe it was the additional oils, who knows, that bitch was as nice as a twenty-six-year-old boat could be without fiberglass. Now we were on a planned course using the East Passage to Newport, then bang a left toward the cape.

It was such a nice day the ocean had about a one and half foot roll to it as we broke the end of the passage. The guy on the boat had never seen the mansions in Newport by the sea before. A slight detour has us checking them out from about a mile distance. They were majestic with the sun hitting them, huge groomed lawns rolling down toward the sea. Alas it was time for the main event, the barge to scuba dive. Three quarters of an hour had us pulling up to the lee side of the barge. That's the side out of the wind and current. We tied up, bow to the barge, stern to the anchor line. As we started gearing up, I ran through the plan. The plan never, ever, to be deviated from. The plan today was to drop to the bottom. After acclimation, start to the rear of the barge because the tide was just starting to come in. It would be easy to start that way as we were totally protected from the incoming tide. The point I made, was to always stay an arms length away, and no more. Rounding the stern would be the current, and one must stay close to the bottom. Also must stay close the broken carcass of the barge. She had hit the reef in the mid nineteen hundreds and broke in half. She still had cement in her holds. How did I know? It was a scary way to find out! Thanks a lot to a dive instructor of mine years ago!

My diving instructor was a fish. No really, I mean this guy was a fish. I had never seen anyone be able to go as far, use as little air, and have so much strength underwater before in my life! We would drift dive through the Westport river while he held the anchor to a fourteen foot Boston whaler. It was incredible fun to get just a little positively buoyant off the bottom, then let the current take over. The best drift dive would be a moon tide going out! Very scenic, and would be an express ride too! You would drift over sunken boats, many lost anchors, and see tons of fish. Some times a stray lobster not expecting a few crazy bastards to be drifting over gave us a show. One thing though, we were always moving too fast to grab them, damn! The dive would have us drift all the way out past Elephant rock at the mouth of the river to the ocean. Depending on the tide we could find ourselves drift to the sunken barge about a mile and a quarter off shore. That's when he told me about a dive we were using the second tanks for this particular day. As always, I'm in! I have nine lives baby!!

The drift dive had been for over an hour from where we started. Coming to the surface had us both screaming a big, 'how's that shit right there!'. That had just been totally fantastic! I felt like I was in a time machine with things flying by in slow motion. Like sky diving in free fall, fucking sideways!! It was the best. We positioned the boat to do another dive at the barge with anchors, and lines to the barge too. This plan we talked about was fucking insane! Your going to, what? Yeah he said we were going down through the engine room.

It had a huge hole at the top to enter. Then, down through the cable crib. He referred to it as, 'lobster alley'! He said the lobsters in there no smarter than a dumb cow that would be in there, waiting for us to grab. We would later indulge at the house. He said after that I could not loose him or turn around. "No turning back at that point, do you hear me!"

We entered the water. Never being inside a wreck before had me more nervous than I would admit. I knew it when I could not raise any spit to rub in my mask to stop it from fogging. Holy shit, I had to talk myself into a zen mode or I would be sucking up air like you read about. Alright now we snorkeled into position above the engine room. Dropping down out of the world we live in, to the other side, the ocean is wild. Now we were in a ripped up engine room. The test of time had all kinds of life attached to any, and everything. We flipped our lights on as now we would be heading down to the cable run. It was the whole length of the barge. About six feet high and four feet wide. Cables attached on the sides of the walls had fallen here and there, all I knew was not to get fucking tangled anywhere. Is this incredible I was thinking. I looked at my compass. Nope, it didn't work! We were in a metal ocean casket right here, 'with one fucking mistake', I was starting to think. Here it is, I can't believe it. It's lobster alley, and it's for frigging real! As we made our way down the cable run the lobsters just kept backing up to get away, there was no way out, other than back by us. He grab bagged ten beauties for the boiling pot later. In minutes we were headed to the one way only, no return!

Here we were at the beginning of the barge storage holds. Eight holds of powdered concrete that never solidified. If things on the bottom silt up, that's like when you raise dust, this stuff was a hundred times worse! A two and a half foot space at the top of the holds between that cloud of death, and the metal ceiling was it! He slid into the first hold, and the end of his fin disappearing is what I saw. That was it! I went straight toward the dusted up maze of a cloud dust raising up with the force of his kicks moving forward. My light needless to say, was not really doing a thing. Bang, I just got to the end of the first bulkhead and the hole to the second wasn't much bigger than two by two feet. I did feel to the right as I entered the second hold and felt what I thought would resemble the center wall of the barge. I was hoping, because my guide was long gone. I know I was starting to suck some air here with a bit of claustrophobic panic! Relax! Oh yeah, here's a wall straight ahead. Same type of hole to exit thank frigging goodness. Coming out of the last bulkhead back into the engine room I was able to see light of the surface again. I knew the rest of the bulkheads could go fuck themselves! I wasn't going! He was waiting in the engine room with a wide eyed reaction to me coming out of the hole. I must have had total fear on my face. He knew I was going to, the prick! Ten lobsters for dinner, yeah!

Now back to this day, we were geared for our dive. We dropped the twenty five feet to the bottom, then continued to the stern of the reef bound barge. A school of fish showed up to see the new comers in their world. I took a knife out to scrape a mussel off the hull and break it, to show him how fast the fish attack an easy meal. Just as I warned him, when we got to the stern the current started. We made our way forward on the sunny side, facing the open ocean too. The current was about six miles per hour I was thinking. It would not be too hard to make an easy trip to the bow of the barge to circumnavigate this thing. We were seeing some ten pound black fish. Damn, I was wishing for a speargun! I had never dove with this guy before so I decided to get to the boat a bit early as to have plenty of air. The most important thing is to stay on the bottom with this current, or your getting swept away. Things were going awesome as we got to the bow. Right as we turned toward the boat, on our home side of the barge, uh oh. I saw him reaching for his leg, and surfacing, I could not catch him.

I have do idea why he thought the surface was the move, but I had a fast decision to make. The first was, let this asshole go! I ran over all the bad circumstances in my head as an outcome in milliseconds. I can't let this guy go, I was just pissed he didn't tell me. If I hadn't saw him, I could have gone in the wrong direction looking for him. I surfaced as well. When I broke the surface we were already about fifteen yards apart. I screamed for him to snorkel straight in toward the barge. If he went for the boat we were screwed, we would get swept away for sure. He was so busy trying to screw with the cramp he didn't want to listen, and did fucking nothing! We were separated by about forty yards now, I would see him every other wave that lifted me or so. Because of the slight delay of not getting right back to the barge we were being swept by the current. I decided since I had about twelve hundred pounds of air left to drop to the bottom and try to make it to the boat. I grabbed a quick compass setting, there would be no surfacing again until I either succeeded or totally fucking failed!

I got to the bottom and grabbed every fucking plant and rock that I could to keep me on the path to my boat. I figured at one point even if I make my anchor line, I'm in! Problem is that the tide and ocean decided that I was not to be a winner. I got to within about seven yards or so to the dive platform of the boat before I almost passed out of hyperventilation. I had used myself up on the bottom against the current, running out of air. The last straw was twenty yards from the boat on the surface, out of energy snorkeling, and not being able to reach her against the tide! The next thing I would do would be to pass out of nitrogen narcosis if I kept going. Drowning was not in this fucking plan! I filled up my buoyancy vest, laid on my back, and started paddling like a Mark Twain riverboat. I was way behind 'mister cramp' and figured his best survival chance was me. I guess because he was acting up and being sorry for himself he never did a thing. I think I must have been really putting it on because I caught up to him, which I never thought I would. I gave him a great, 'your an asshole' speech and then showed him in two easy seconds how to get rid of the cramp. Now we had been drifting for quite a while, and the sun was setting.

It can be summer and you can be wearing a wet suit, but hypothermia will be setting in. I was starting to do the old body shiver that you cannot stop. He was cold too, I could tell by the thin blue lips he was sporting. I asked if he had a flash light, like you should always dive with. Thank you I grabbed it and put it in my vest so he would not loose it. I figured in a few hours we would be hitting the Cape Cod Canal. That's when the flash lights could come in handy to get us rescued. I will tell you this, I cannot for the life of me figure out why the nine boats that went by us never noticed the waiving of two scuba divers with a circle above their heads. It's a symbol of assistance needed! They had to be drinking, or just stupid. I can't believe it's more dark than sunset now, it's been hours drifting. Now you could hear an engine coming. It was coming in the direction heading toward us, nearing the canal entrance. This fucking dude was flying! I grabbed the two flash lights and started pointing them in that direction. I figured even a stoned drunk would see them. My life was counting on it! I made a quick crack, I think it was nervous comedy. I remember screaming "full speed ahead, fuck the swimmers! Hey, hey, what the hell!" He went flying by us. It was a Formula thirty five foot ocean race boat just heading out for a screwed up joy ride. After strafing us he entered the canal. We were about to drift through the canal also! The current was about twenty miles per hour now, holy shit!

I guess us two screaming at the asshole in the Formula, disturbed an old couple sitting on their new boat near the Lobster Pot restaurant. They showed up to ask us if we knew we couldn't scuba dive in the canal. I told them they were a great sight for sore cold people that had been drifting for hours! They were some cool old people for sure. They were all in to bring me back to my boat tonight with the promise of being able to guide them back. I cannot know why this old guy would put his faith is some fucking jerk that just drifted up! He let me have the reins of his new little Bay Liner and I snapped us back to my boat with very little fan fair. I got my boat running and guided him back to the canal entrance, where they found us. He would not even consider taking the nice tip I had. He saved our asses that night! With their hugs and goodbyes, 'Mr. cramp' and I had a long, slow nice evening cruise to the East Passage back to my mooring in Tiverton. I still always call that asshole, 'Mr. Cramp!'

HIT JOB
SHE DID IT

Get him exactly to the plan, then walk away slow! Oh yeah CW was getting it! This all got planned just to put the ultimate 'hit job' on him. Years before, our band decided to invest in a few private parties a year. The regular club venues were great. Occasional claim to fame fronting for a few celebrity bands was keeping us busy for sure. We decided if the band threw their own parties, we could do crazy shit, and make more money too. Now it was just a matter of the holidays coming to pick for the party dates. My brother CW and I picked the list, now it was onto finding the club owner to go with the deal. Not every club had dates open, or they were out right afraid of what could happen! This was turning out to not be easy. I had a stroke of luck for one of our first parties using the NCO club at the Guard Unit I was currently operating from. I was hoping this would go well. I invited plenty of people from the unit coming back from overseas deployments. I had just got back in country myself with fanfare and excitement a few days before. Yeah, I had been planning this one for months. I ran the NCO club too, so we were very motivated to say the least. People needed to blow off some steam. Some of the troops had been in dry countries besides, what more can I tell you there!

My plan was to have a nice cheap meal, great comedy, and my band play to cap it off. Hopefully when all was said and done, I would make some cash too. It didn't take much effort at all to sell over one hundred and seventy five tickets for this spaghetti dinner dance. I noticed the list of ticket buyers that followed the band. Wow, I could not believe my brother had the balls to invite four girls that he was dating. Yeah four! He used to date about six at once, usually. He would give them all the same frigging gifts, wrapped the same at the holidays. He even called them all the same nicknames. I guess you'd call that something technically, I just called it 'masterful'! Seeing the names on the list had me going in for the jugular here. My parents would attend all events that were special. They always got the royal treatment at the gigs. This one had them sitting at the center table, center front near the dance floor. The best table in the house. Five or so of our family and friends sat with them. Now with that said, this is where it's going to get interesting. As you say, 'I surrounded them with excitement' to come.

I decided to seat all the chicks my brother had invited to the party in a nice semi circle of tables right around my mother's. I thought they would all be vying for her attention. I would have a blast watching CW shit himself while trying to play the gig! I damn well knew for sure he wasn't going to spend much time at the tables on break this night. This had potential to be fucking great! Coming back from overseas it was awesome to see everyone. I had missed playing in the band too. Having these two different worlds of mine collide in the same room was great too. Think about it, the band crowd, and my military buddies all at once. I was hoping the cops didn't get involved! The meal had a ton of comedy being served at the chow line. I know a few meat balls were tossed around too. I got hit with one! I got up to do some comedy for a few minutes as the band was getting ready to come on. That's when it happened! Oh my word, the back ground music started a buddy John had set up with my brother. I was happy they had at least let me tell a few jokes first, but now this was going to be a pisser. Here we go!

The music playing had a Saudi Arabian feel to it. Any second, you thought belly dancers were coming out. I hadn't hired any, that I could remember anyway. At one point I was talking about hiring strippers and shit until I realized too many, 'nice' people were coming. Not just the fun crowd! The announcer came over the PA, and wouldn't you know, it's 'Sheikh Ala-Mony'! A man started coming into the club from the kitchen. He was dressed in perfect traditional garb from over seas. Holy crap, it was John. He came out slowly, as the crowd came to their feet laughing and cheering him on. Let's say this, John never needs edging on! After all the appropriate hand gestures he had me ready to piss my self. Then he said under his breath to ask him shit, we were about to wreck this fuckin' joint! The funny part about this shit is John's wife had just whacked him with divorce papers days before. The outfit was just a souvenir, but now it was being put to use! The alimony lines worked so well that day with that Sheikh outfit on. I sit here laughing my ass off thinking about it. The band finally went on that night, we even had John come up and sing some 'Sheikh-Ala-Mony' blues! It was great, he was a funny bastard! My brother only had a few close calls with three of his girlfriends talking to my mother at break. Yeah, he just went hitting on one of the girls in the guard unit. What a dog!

The next major holiday coming this time was Valentines day. It was going to be at a club in Pawtucket, Rhode Island. This place could do about three hundred in the joint, and it was free to me! I did business with the manager that ran the place, selling him cars. The only thing to do was leave it clean and packed up like you found it, he'd make his money on the bar. That ticket was hot, as I sold the party out before the holidays. I had an extra plan to make some big cash also, and this was a frigging beauty. Again on the guest list I saw the names. My crazy bastard brother was inviting all six girl-friends to the party! Now, I was going to get his ass this time I hope. The tickets were really expensive. We thought not many would come being Valentine's day so we'd maximize. Instead, everybody came it was great. I had noticed CW hitting on this chick the weekend before the party in Boston. Yeah, he didn't know, I took the time to double around behind him and ask her to help me out. I got her number, and in the middle of telling her how she was going to get the 'same' things the other six do, she was in! I set up the plan for the party. Oh yeah, she was going to be coming too!

The band was all full of excitement on this night, and the place was packed. Tickets were being sold for raffles on over thirty things I had businesses donate. All profit and, wait there's more! I decided to get lobsters for a, 'Louie the Lobster' raffle for five lobsters! Tickets to be drawn at end of first set break. I could not believe I made way over a frigging grand selling the tickets alone on break. I was sell-ing tickets for five bucks an arms length, they all went fast. I spent twenty five bucks for the lobsters and raked it in. I had the special plan though for the 'new' girlfriend. I had let her use my car for the caper. I had put her up in a hotel so I could give her a ride back to Boston the next day. "Here's the plan", I told her. "I will call you when we are almost going back on for the second set. I will talk him into playing this song."

I told her when, and exactly how this had to work. If she did anything different, shit could really go wrong! The big thing I explained, was how not to give attention to yourself. "It's just like that, get in the car and go! I will see you at the room later." This chick did pretty frigging good job when you come to think about it. She did it for spite, and a hundred bucks!

The first band break was like a mania selling tickets, and seeing old friends. I kept looking around hoping I wasn't going to see, 'her' too early to screw this thing up. I heard the magic words, 'saddle up' across the crowd from the PA. That was our signal to the stage to play another set. I grabbed my phone and put the plan in motion. It was like if there 'was' a grassy knoll, it was in this place fifteen minutes from now! I cautiously got to the stage. On the way I made sure the back hall was clear, and nothing was in the way. I may need an escape here. All the six of CW's girls at this party had no idea about 'the new one'! Just as planned, the second song I begged him to play, he did. It was perfect for him to show off anyway. I picked 'Pretty Woman', for the attack. There were reasons. One, the dance floor would be absolutely rocking with every one who could even move on it. Two, because he would be so busy singing the end of the song, he'd never see the one who 'did' it. Yeah it was perfect. Right after the part he gets the crowd stomping their feet on the floor going crazy. That's when you make the move toward the stage through the center of the dance floor. Just slightly push anyone out of the way, they are all expecting body contact. As the band goes into the last phrase, hit him on the word 'pretty'!

I've seen snipers not have her timing. It was perfect! Right as he sang the tag out of 'Pretty Woman' at the end of the song, we never heard 'woman'! Oh yeah this chick slithered right through the crowd with a nice huge cream pie for an assault weapon. On the open mouth of 'pretty', she got him perfectly in the puss! She turned really slow and slid away, without being noticed as the one that popped him with the pie! Wow, there must have been a little animosity there. The cream went all over the drums after it cracked him. I just knew the music stopped fast. CW took his eye glasses off and looked into the crowd. As he took the eyeglasses off, nice clean rings around his eyes made me laugh like hell. He just automatically said, "Ger!" He didn't get the rest of my name out when I knew it was time for the fast escape route! I ran out to the car I had used to get him fresh clothes, and face cloth that were ready to clean up. He showed outside and I was laughing so fucking hard he couldn't beat me down. He started laughing too until we almost were in tears! I wished him a happy fucking birthday, and told him I loved him. Laughing like Hyenas, I told him the kick about it was, that his new chick had done the 'Hit Job'! Ahhhhhahaha!

YOU AGAIN
HOW COULD IT HAPPEN

Crash, the sink broke off the wall! At least, that's what I think I heard in that bathroom. That all started when a customer of mine kept asking to go out with someone at the store. I told him no about a thousand times. He kept putting in huge orders at the store just to talk to her. I have to say I didn't care, I needed the commissions. I guess it was a huge job he was working on, almost across the road from the store. All I know is this guy just kept coming in for this, or that, just to be there. Finally it came to me fixing him up for the lunch date. This had to be out of control because both of them were married. This time I guess I wasn't the perfect, how you say, marriage counselor. The set up was in!

The lunch date came. He showed up really not dressed for construction. Dan had on a 'job interview' suit. My buddy Bob and I kind of laughed as we knew what was going down. They were finally stepping out for the lunch date. I had fixed Jen and Dan up for the deal. She was in the ladies room doing the last minute tidy up, and we sicked him in there on her. They were so smitten with each other it seemed funny to us to watch it all. They were like two school kids.

I guess it's really because they were both married. I have to say she came in that day looking exquisite. So there they were talking as she was finishing up when I heard the door close. Uh oh, I think he just went in there. Bob and I started laughing like hell. It couldn't have been more than two minutes when that sink came crashing off the wall. The door opened and I got an assistance call to the ladies room from Dan. Ten minutes had us in there laughing our fool asses off as we got the sink fixed. I told him to please go take a massive crazy 'lunch' date and make it for all it was worth. They did obviously because that kept going on long after I was gone from that store. I went back to the band and car business, as always.

One day, while in my office one Saturday morning, I was nursing one of the big hangovers from playing in the band the night before. Usually on a day like that, everybody knew I was useless. At least until after three pukes in the basket, and lunch finally staying down anyway. I couldn't believe this lady didn't want to leave my office. She came in while I think I was unconscious actually. When I got myself in order enough to realize what the hell was going on, I was the overflow guy and they were busy out there. They just kind of dumped her in my office and told her good luck! Oh sorry, as I got myself going and ready for action. She jumped into the situation. She was trading a paid off car and wanted something to piss her husband off! Wow, that fucking woke me up. "What? To piss your husband off", I remember asking her. Oh yeah, she said that he had been screwing around, and now it was her turn to have some fun. I could not get my dealer plate out of my desk fast enough. It didn't take much to put her in a car that would definitely piss him off come the night he finally saw it!

I'm sure that car pissed him off because she kept coming to see the band I was playing in to tell me about it. I will say this, that went way too far also! Things be as they may, life goes on. Years later I decided to blast off from the car biz again for another stint into the wild unknown. It seemed like every switch in management had me doing this. I told them I would be back when they were done screwing around. Half way home the phone rang and I couldn't believe it was Bob. I worked with him at that store when Dan and Jen had the, 'sink incident'! After catching up, and laughing once more about the sink falling off the damn wall, he got to the point. Working for a finish construction company going around to be an 'A' Team supposedly. I was already suspect but since I had just quit a job an hour before, I figured this was luck. "Yeah, when?" He said, "see you at nine tonight!" I asked, "What?" "Yeah we're doing a mall near not far from Boston and it's overnight, be ready at eight!" he said.

I couldn't believe I was getting fucking construction hand tools together after years in the car biz. Here we go again. The truck pulled up and it was the same old crazy bastard Bob I had known years before. This fucking guy just don't age. He was ten years my senior, but obviously did more to take care of himself and shit. I was overweight and couldn't believe I was going to do this shit again. He started laughing and with all the jokes of forgetting more than they know, I went on to do several years at that construction company. That company had it's characters, and they all had their jobs. One thing was always finding someone you had some common interests. You really found out what common interests you have when you end up working out of town, stranded. Not really stranded, but working long hours four days a week, and the drive being too far to get there every day. Now to find a hotel that will have five to eight construction guys, and not bitch. A bit of scouting found one for us.

Bob and I went along to jobs ourselves and tried not to get involved on the big jobs with that company. We figured we could get things done quicker to be home earlier, and be closer to home all the time. Finally these schools had to be finished in Connecticut and we had to go. The job started before the end of school year, with any luck we could be out of there before snow fell again. Here comes some craziness. I got there fashionably late as usual. I had to, I rode with Bob and we rushed for fucking no one. We hit the coffee places on the way there, and got the rooms at the motel booked before heading to the job. When we got there all the normal 'late' ball busting went on, like they thought I would really care. I got told though how I would be working with Wade. Wade? Yeah, he doesn't like to work with anyone. Your it! Good luck. I really need that laboratory cabinetry to happen today so, please. Just get it done and there he is in there, again, good luck. Then I heard the door slam shut behind me.

I got some of my tools prepped for the job at hand. I couldn't even see this person I was supposedly going to be working with. Yo! Wade! I heard a low grumble from the back corner of the classroom behind a mound of cabinet boxes. "Go away." I think that's what I remember him saying. If it wasn't it may have been a bit more colorful. "Naw, I'm staying and we're either going to do this together or we make break every cabinet in this fucking room, but I'm staying!" "Suit yourself and go fuck yourself", or something to that effect came out of him. Well I think after we talked shit for a while and I may even have swatted him at one point. He laughed and said that's how his kids would hit him. We ended up deciding exactly how to muckle this job and be onto the next. Let's put it this way, there was a lot of money being handed around at the coffee truck on lost bets of either one of us knocking the other out before morning break. Instead we came laughing, got our shit at the truck and were on our way. We are still great friends today. 'That guy's just not right', is what Wade's old man would say about me after hearing of some of the race trips, and dating stories. Every time I had a chance when we met, it was time to catch up with the latest. The man loved to laugh, Russ, bless your soul!

I had the best tickets in NASCAR and extra ones too. It was time to get Wade a cheap bike and head to the races. Bristol, Tennessee was the destination, and a mountain journey on the way. What are the odds of my race buddy in South Carolina finding a bike in Warwick, Rhode Island not more than thirty miles from me. I had already woken Wade in the middle of the night a few times with a potential find I had came up with. I would say "I found one, it's a road trip but it'll be worth it." The next thing I would hear from him would be, "Ger, it's fucking three thirty and I get up in another hour for work." Uh oh, you mean I did it again? I would get lost in time on the computer and then make the call, jeez it was always so late. This time though Brian down south found this one online. Wade left work after lunch the next day so we could make a rendezvous to look at the bike. I listened to the guy's wife yelling at us through the window not to sell it for our offer. I figured he didn't care if she laid him much anyway, he didn't listen to her one bit. I do remember taking his tags off the thing and magic marking 'BR549' where the plate would have been. Yeah Jr. Samples from Hee Haw used that selling his used cars, it was good enough for us! Wade jumped on it and drove it home with no helmet, no plates, no back brakes, and a low tire! Laughing like hell we went to eat and make our plan for the upcoming trip.

Two weeks went by fast, and now it was time to launch on our adventure. The morning I pulled up to his house, Wade was putting the finishing tune up touches on the bike he had just resurrected from the dead. Now it had brakes, a great tune up and she was ready to go. A fantastic tasty tidbit came up though. That week when he was getting the bike ready cleaning it, the neighbor became interested in talking. It was a big 'YOU Again', as Wade's neighbor had sold that bike to the guy in Warwick we had just bought it from! Yes, it was the early ninety's and the bike only had about a hundred and eighty more miles on it than the guy bought it with. He said he was too scared to drive it. Now it was our time to hit the road. We blasted off out though the back roads of Rhode Island to the highways heading south. We made Virginia that night to have dinner, drinks and laugh at some crazy stories. The next morning had us heading up into the mountains to observe some sights! Then it was to make our way south, to meet up with the crowd of my southern race friends.

It happened again at about the second overlook. A covering of beautiful butterflies landed all over the bikes, us, and everywhere. That made the Skyline drive start with a bang that morning and the day never let up. The sights were awesome, the weather was perfect for the motorcycles heading to the races baby! We felt like movie stars with the camping area welcome! My group of race buddies had a whole section of a camp area. It was nice to have a place to hang before heading to the races and after also. Just southern great times making ice cream home made and great food on the grill too. Many jokes at the portable john late that evening about shot gun shells found on sight by one guy. Wade and I just almost laughed our asses off to think of the shit that guy had just come out with. It was conversation still today we laugh about. It was even more interesting to get in the pre race betting pool. The guy putting it together really didn't want to let the 'yanks' in the thing. All my race buddies vouched for us, and we were in the pool. I picked a guy I had never heard of, and I followed the sport closely. Wade went on to immediately piss off about forty other rebels in an instant when he picked Dale Jr.! Now they hated him in the campsite. Yeah we were in Earnhardt country here, I think Wade could have sold that pick! My obscure pick was the first out of the race so I won. The best part was Dale Jr. won also! When the rebel came to pay off my buddy he said, "YOU Again!" Another laugh when we got to the room that night, 'YOU Again!' as we laughed our asses off counting the money!

A few months later the company got a job to do a restaurant. The problem was the building not being ready for the finish work. Another problem was the timing. It was almost supposed to be open. Worst thing they could have done was let me and Wade work together. We had a lot of jokes for rain hitting you while running a table saw, standing in two inches of water. We also were relentless with the superintendent on the job. He was from New Jersey and had the worst wig you could find. A two year old would be calling that one out! Wade and I just beat this guy up on the cut metal to make the building four feet too short. Hence no room for all the HVAC, or we could just leave our four feet of finish work out, and laugh our asses off again. Or maybe the tile guy from New Jersey falling asleep on the floor on the wet tile mortar overnight. There was always something. He just started walking the other way if he saw us coming. The look on the superintendent's face was precious when he saw the fire retardant wall panels in the kitchen. They were just sliding down off the walls down onto the floor because it had started raining like hell, and naturally the roof wasn't tight yet. I think one of the last straws for him was when we asked him if the finish package used A/C sheets of lumber core for the walls. We told him they had shipped B/B/S. Just so you know there is no such category. When he asked, "B/B/S?" He got the answer. Yeah this stuff was 'bad both sides'! He really didn't want to talk to us after that!

The press to finish the building for restaurant to open was in full force. We called in some extra help from a temporary job source company. The two carpenters that came had one looking familiar to me. I started telling Wade about the store I worked where Bob and I set up the construction guy with the chick. Wade almost dropped the cabinet we were installing when I told him about the 'sink incident'! Now I had to confirm it was him. I called Bob across the room. When he answered his phone he looked at me, I gave him the point to meet me outside. We confirmed that was the same guy. I can't believe we have Dan here as we started laughing. We both decided not to talk about the 'sink' so we could get this job done. Now my phone kept ringing, it was an old friend with a problem to solve.

Needless to say Wade was doing a whole lot of wondering what the hell was going on. We hadn't installed anything in an hour between all the laughing and phone calls. My bud on the other end of the line was explaining how the drummer in their three piece band had to go. He went on further to explain that it was more complicated. The drummer was a cousin to the other guy in the band. At this point, I was already backing out figuring this would be a battle every night instead of fun. He then explained that the other guy is the one who wanted the drummer gone. So let me get this straight, "he wants to blow his cousin off?" Yep, he then went on to the reasons. I cut him short because Wade was standing there, just looking at his work partner shooting the shit on the phone. The plan was, if I said yes they'd call him now to fire him. Then, they would move his drums out of the dive bar they were currently playing that afternoon. Nice, I got off the phone and told Wade I would be drumming at a dive in Fall River that Friday night. I started telling him how the cousins weren't getting along, so my buddy was making the call to the guy to fire him now. It was at this point that we were going to need some extra assistance for a lift of large box cabinets for install overhead. I called Dan to help. We were already having an undercurrent of laughter starting. I know it had to be the 'sink' story I shared with Wade when I saw Dan that morning.

The next scene had the three of us lifting a monster cabinet for the install. Perfect timing had Dan's phone ringing the second we were done. Dan started to tell the person on the other end of the line some things that made you go hum! Wade and I just looked at each other and almost started to laugh when the line came up I couldn't believe I heard. Dan told the person on the phone they had better not damage his drums if they move them out of the club. As he was hanging up the phone he was starting to tell me the story how he had been playing drums with his cousin in a band. He didn't get along at all with my friend so as he was starting to say his name, my phone rang. Excuse me, hate to cut you short but I had a call. When I answered my buddy said right off the bat, so Friday you're in. He gave me the name of the club and time. I asked Dan if it was at all possible in the world for it to happen that he would be working with the guy taking his drum gig that Friday. We were astounded to think that the world could be so small. I really roughed up his mind when I asked if he ever had a, 'sink incident', in a store bathroom. Yeah, at that point he just said, "YOU Again!" Oh yeah baby, it's me again. That day in the parking lot when he was leaving I asked Dan if his ex wife drove a particular kind of vehicle. Oh shit Dan was about to ask, when I told him I sold it to her. I had left the car biz to come work for this company. Both of us were laughing, but before Dan drove away his window came down. He asked me to give him some warning next time. That way he wouldn't have to figure it out for himself and scream, "YOU Again!!" Yes it was!

FIREWORKS
LIFE'S DISPLAY

I bet you can remember the first time you saw them. The huge thud caught your attention, but the next thing scared the shit out of you! That big bright crash of light in the night sky followed by the boom you could feel. The babies in the crowd started crying their fool heads off. If it was a good one it got crowd reaction for sure. As you got older they got better. Maybe it was the location, or the event, it may have just been the company of your companion. Every display though, was their own, no two being the same. I think the same about the twenty two thousand eight hundred plus days on this rotating huge ball going around the sun. No two have ever really been the same. Blessed as I may be though, I really don't think it could have been scripted. Even if you could touch up the x-rays you couldn't have made it better. The lighting of the wick was, believe it or not, St. Patrick's Day to be born on Christmas. Oh yeah don't think that was so easy. She fell down the stairs and also off the Darby horses at Crescent Park while pregnant with me. Born with a forceps black eye, I've always blamed everything on those events. In the preceding chapters all were part of the display of life's fireworks.

Pipeline, could symbolize the beginning of the underwater wick burning so slowly one couldn't see the movement of the burn, just the bright flare. CW took me into the world of music where I met some of the best people I have ever known. The musicians he introduced me to that are like brothers from different mothers. I guess we all have a sick demented way of looking at life. My life was enriched totally by these people. Without Earl, I wouldn't have known the noise I made in the garage at their break on his drums that night would change my life. It still does today with his wisdom in all our conversations. It goes further, his famous artist son Brian's advice for the cover of this book. Without Nino, I wouldn't know the fun of playing so many gigs a week. My brother and I were always ready, but to find someone to go with us, yeah baby! Without Matt, I wouldn't have experienced someone jumping off my drum stage every night. I wouldn't have a beautiful old wooden rocking horse made for his first born and used by all the rest, under a Christmas tree in Michigan every year. Maybe the next generation are riding it now. The wick, my friends is burning slowly. Without Eddie, life could have been totally different, if not ended. He was always in the right places, and always making a call for some reason at the most critical moments. There has to something to the day he played a certain lick on CW's guitar, then Matt called right at that moment. Oh yeah, and the day for surgery check in. I had to have a ride naturally, but to let Eddie near the check in window was an error. He told the lady my name and said, "he is checking in for the lobotomy!" She was so NOT amused and I couldn't stop laughing, so correcting him was impossible. We went directly to the Irish Bar on Mission Hill, beer and burgers for a great recovery!

As a firework launches out of the tube, life brought chapter Tina. She was the pet a kid grows up with that would exemplify, 'best friend'. Some of the fun moments as a kid looking at the sky with her laying there, having her love all the way to entry into the Air Force. Along the fireworks' express route to the sky chapter Max or Maureen and Keep 'Em would be in full force pushing the bounds of growing up. The chapter The Braga showed how much life can happen around one item in your view every day, just as watching the trace of the sparks go up in the sky. Slowly rising still, chapter Until They Come would apply as it would be important to watch all the signs of what could be. As the trace of the firework continues up into the sky came chapter I'll Take a Box, and life was starting to really explode at this time. The band was rocking in full force and a turn was about to take place.

Boom, smash and crash with unbelievable force, light and sparks came chapter Riding Free~Fall, just like the firework making it's way out into the night sky. Spreading out into the world and finding out how the others live was an eye opening experience. Chapter, Let ME Drive would widen the world even further. I learned about other people from Tennessee and from Oklahoma. It showed me how big the world was. Chapter, Makin' it Back taught you to just put faith in God. There is no other path! So the big streaks in the night sky sparkle and shine as the fireworks life is at it's climax. Chapter, Hot Fun is just life being at it's best. A beautiful summer night but without survival having to kick in quick, life would be boring! That's where chapters, The Barge and Bernie come into play. Both being survival battles, again it's like the firework could have burned out!

As the finale of the display comes, there were chapters like Blood Brothers, that teach you that you don't know who your talking to all the time. So treat every one like you want to be treated, they could be sent to you by an angel. The chapter, Hit Job just showed how much fun a musician can actually have with life. Life is a blast!!

We used to say, 'and get paid for this too?'! God bless you CW you are severely missed. I miss the daily phone calls with a joke, or just the onstage abuse! I wish I could endure it just once more! I would give anything for it. Like the firework that has disbursed and burnt away, there is no more but the memory. The memories thank goodness that you always photographed while playing any instrument you played. Up came the camera with a flash when you least expected it. I walk through the house looking at the pictures of it all. I walk through the yard and look at the trees you and I planted my friend. I was so small the holes to plant them you dug were huge to me. Now some are over one hundred feet tall. I will guard this place with my life and leave as you CW, Mom and Dad did, feet up! I thank you God for a great fun incredible free falling life. It was always, Full Speed Ahead!! Screw the Swimmers!!

ABOUT THE AUTHOR

Gerry Benoit a product of Somerset, Massachusetts. Lead and background vocalist drummer for over three decades in a Classic hits band. A graduate of the Air Force School of Applied Aerospace Sciences, serving in Special Forces Combat Communications for almost a decade. Auto Sales for many years give a background of stories for a lifetime. He scuba dove the whole east coast to the Yucatan. Competitive in tennis, bowling and can work wonders on a pool table. Supports rescue 'Brittany Spaniel' dogs. He never rides faster than his angels either!